THE EMPTIED HEART

A Father's Memoir

THE
EMPTIED
HEART

a father's memoir

by

RONALD TALNEY

PORTLAND·OREGON
INKWATERPRESS.COM

Publisher: Inkwater Press | www.inkwaterpress.com

ISBN-13 978-1-62901-650-4 | ISBN-10 1-62901-650-0

1 3 5 7 9 10 8 6 4 2

For Linnette, for Jennifer, for Aaron,
and, of course,
for Allison

So tell us
that we loved her;
that we were held on her word's edge
as if by magic;
that somewhere mountains rise,
casting shadows like a weight,
splitting the earth
with her incredible silence
and we will whisper "daughter," "sister,"
out upon this
gathering of darkness.

"The bridge between the known and the unknown is always love."

Stephen Levine, Author,
Who Dies?

"You cannot bring back what is lost; you can only mark the place where absence reigns."

Vera Schwarcz
Bridge Across Broken Time

"How shall the heart be reconciled to its feast of losses?

Stanley Kunitz
The Layers

FOREWORD

THIS IS THE ACCOUNT OF A DEATH. THE DEATH OF OUR daughter. It is also an account of survival. And not merely the survival of individuals but of that separate entity we call "a couple." It has been well documented that a very high percentage of bereaved parents eventually divorce or separate following the death of their child, no matter the cause. My wife, Linnette, and I were determined not to let that happen to us following the death of our child. This is the story of that death, that effort, and of that survival.

It is not our intention to be critical of those who have shared this experience and whose marriages or relationships have not survived the stresses and strains of that loss. We fully understand how that can happen. Rather it is merely to document our own effort and to perhaps give hope to others who may unfortunately find they too are struggling to live with such a loss. To paraphrase the poet, Theodore Roethke, we learn by going where we have to go. Everyone so affected must ultimately find his or her own way, but I hope this account will shed light on that journey. It will not make the journey any less painful, but perhaps it might make it more bearable.

PROLOGUE

"Each of us has his own rhythm
of suffering."

Roland Barthes, *Mourning Diary*

IT IS MID-JUNE. I AM SITTING BY THE FRONT WINDOW LOOKING
*out at the sidewalk. Early morning sunlight pours in, filtered
through the branches of our dogwood tree, and spreads
its designs across the carpet at my feet. Children are running past the house on their way to school, their last day of
classes. They are lugging book-packs on their backs. Some
are carrying lunch boxes. They are laughing and pushing
one another, unaware that I am watching. One boy grabs
another's hat and tosses it across the lawn like a Frisbee.
The other boy retrieves it and chases his tormentor.*

*I sip hot coffee and stare after them as they quickly
disappear from sight, past our hedge and around the
corner. The sounds of laughter trail after them. And
now I can hear Linnette moving about in the bedroom
upstairs, dressing for work, preparing to come down. For
her too, as a teacher, it is, finally, the end of the school
year, the end of what has now become for her a daily
torture.*

Perhaps she will ask me, "How did you sleep?" and I will answer with a question of my own, "How do you think I slept?" And she will nod, as she always does, and make herself a piece of toast and a cup of tea and sit across from me, and I will look into her tired eyes, those deep, dark circles of loss that mark her face, and marvel at the fact that she is with me still.

Or perhaps she will say, "I think I feel a little better this morning," and I will wonder how she could possibly think so. Or she might ask, "Do you have to be in court this morning?" And I will stare at her, not entirely sure where I am supposed to be this morning. Or why. Or for whom. Or, looking out the window at the blue sky and the sunlight still streaming in, I might say, "I hope you can enjoy your last day of classes," and she will turn away, thinking me insensitive, crass, or even cruel. We now live in a world where we are constantly caught between love and anger, between emotional distance and our continuing need for one another. We live in a world where even the smallest of small talk exposes the vast gulf that now, at times, divides us.

This morning it has been nine weeks to the day since the accident in which our daughter Allison was killed. This morning, as with every morning, we waken to her death again. And again. This is how we mark each new day, each week, each month. So far we have survived, if living like this could be called survival. We now occupy a space where we live together as a couple, but apart and lonely at the same time. We have become, as the psychologists have defined it, "bereaved parents." At times we move in our separate worlds like robots. We touch but are often numb to each other. We speak and our estranged voices assault the stillness that surrounds us and echoes throughout the empty house as if across a void.

But even now somehow we sense, despite what and whom we have lost that we cannot live in this state of suspended agony forever. Each new day we are slowly learning the lessons of grief, those lessons that tell us a heart cannot burn with such pain forever. It will then either be destroyed by the flames or it will become stronger than it would otherwise have been. It may become, in time, an "emptied heart," as the German writer Hermann Hesse has called it, a wounded heart made of a porcelain so delicate but so strong it can survive the fire that made it to become more beautiful than it was. That which was superficial will have been burned away. That which remains is a heart not free of love but perfected by loss.

"Hold nothing dear and you will have nothing to lose," says a character in a novel by Remarque. I look at Linnette. She looks at me. And somehow across this room, across all our tortured days and nights, we still cling to one another. Despite all that has happened we still weave a common history. Even now we sense in some deep place, beneath the tears and pain, the emptied heart has everything to lose.

CHAPTER ONE

IT IS THE EARLY MORNING HOURS OF FRIDAY, APRIL 8, 1988. A small sports car is speeding north on the New Jersey Turnpike toward New York City. A young man in his mid-twenties is driving. Curled up on the seat next to him dozing is a slender young blonde-haired woman of twenty-three. I imagine music playing on the radio or from a tape player. Janis Joplin, perhaps. A favorite of hers. Or Kris Kristofferson. "Me and Bobby McGee." I imagine the young man gazing into the darkness that surrounds them, tapping the steering wheel in time to the music. A light rain is falling. There is just a hint of dawn light beginning to tease the eastern skyline. Another hour and they should be home.

It has been a long trip, one that started in New York City, down through New Jersey to Pennsylvania at the request of the young man's parents, and now they are on their return trip. The parents live in Brooklyn. The young man is single and lives with them. They had asked him to

1

drive down into Pennsylvania to close up their vacation home. The task completed, instead of staying the night and resting, they decide to return to New York. He wants to get home in time to get some sleep before having to report to his job at John F. Kennedy International Airport where he is employed as a mechanic, part of the ground maintenance crew for Trans World Airlines. The young woman, also single, her blonde hair highlighted by the glow of the dash lights, sleeping now beside him, also works for Trans World Airlines. She is a flight attendant. She has a late flight scheduled to London. She had agreed to keep him company on his trip into Pennsylvania and back. She shares an apartment on Long Island with other flight attendants, and her roommates will be expecting her.

As the Turnpike enters the city of Secaucus, just across the river from New York City, for reasons we will never know, the car suddenly swerves out of control, sideswipes the center guardrail, careens wildly across three lanes of traffic, strikes the guardrail on the other side, becomes airborne, flies over 130 feet, and crashes finally into a tree. Neither occupant is wearing a seatbelt. The young man is thrown from the car. He suffers massive head injuries but will survive. The young woman is also thrown from the car and with tremendous force strikes the tree. Instinctively she draws herself into a fetal position at the side of the road and by the time emergency vehicles and police arrive she is dead.

It is 3:45 a.m., E.S.T.

CHAPTER TWO

It is Friday, April 8, 1988. Linnette and I are awake at the usual time to get ready for work. It is a sunny day and, with the end of the workweek fast approaching, we are looking forward to a relaxing weekend. It has been a busy week and we both feel the need to kick back and put our feet up. Perhaps we will go for an early spring hike in the Columbia River Gorge. Perhaps a leisurely drive to the coast. Our children almost grown, we are now on the verge of being "empty nesters." Our oldest daughter Jennifer is married and in graduate school in Portland, Oregon, where we live. Our son Aaron is an undergraduate student in Seattle at the University of Washington.

And Allison, our middle child? The "Sky Girl?" Who knows where she is at the moment. She is a flight attendant for Trans World Airlines, based in New York City. We call her our Sky Girl. We spoke to her by telephone just two days ago. She called from her apartment on Long Island to ask how to cook fish. She was cooking dinner for her landlord, Mike. She spoke of leaving for London today. Or was it Paris? We can hardly keep up with her comings and goings. In a little over three years with the airline she has experienced more of the world than we will probably ever know.

She was the rebellious one. Our designated kid from hell. A pain in the rumpolla, as Linnette often put it. A beautiful baby. A charming and delightful toddler. But once she hit middle school and high school. Look out. From then on, she was a challenge to our parenting. This was the child who defied us when at age thirteen we said of course she could not go to Seattle with friends and no adult supervision and in the middle of a school week to attend a Grateful Dead concert. Of course, she went anyway. She climbed out her second-story bedroom window in the middle of the night, dropped down to the roof of the attached garage, shinnied down a tree, met up with her friends, took a Greyhound bus to Seattle and went to the concert anyway. We were frantic.

This is the child who at age fifteen refused to live with us any longer and went to live at her best friend's home across the street, a large family with six children. She had decided the rules in our home were too strict. Suzanne's mother called to tell us Allison was there when she failed to come home. She told us not to worry, that when it came to raising children she had dealt with everything short of murder or mayhem. After six weeks avoiding us except when the grandparents were visiting for some special occasion, she returned home when she realized the rules in Suzanne's house were even more strictly enforced than in ours.

This is the child who liked to wear a pin, except when

4

her grandparents were present, that read "Give me a Fucking Break!" For awhile it seemed to be her favorite accessory, along with a vintage feather boa, the beaded handbag, the floppy hat, the strapless dress with sequins, and the spiked high heels. This was what she might wear to school. When she went to school. But this is also the child who would often sneak over to her grandparents' house early in the morning and leave a single rose on their doorstep.

Jennifer and Aaron were goal-oriented and content to engage in the usual teenage escapades, and happy to enjoy college life and prepare for professional careers. Allison was discontented with school and with the confinements of day-to-day life. She longed to spread her wings. And she did. By becoming a flight attendant for an international airline.

I remember initially planting the idea. Linnette and I were returning from an exhausting trip to South America and were on the last leg of our journey from Miami to Portland. After the rather haphazard trip north from Peru on the Peruvian airline I saw how capable and professional the flight attendants on American Airlines appeared to be. I noticed in particular how the flight attendants seemed to take pride in their duties, how they handled the needs of passengers, never seeming to be rattled by requests or demands for service. Allison had been doing public contact work in restaurants and shopping mall stores while taking some classes at Mt. Hood Community College. She was always at her best when she was working. Even in high school it had been that way. If nothing else, she always took work seriously. I remember turning to Linnette and saying something to the effect that Allison would be perfect in a job like this. Linnette agreed.

Some time later I saw an article in the newspaper about TWA recruiting flight attendants locally. I cut out the article and left it on Allison's bed. I knew from experience that if I brought up the subject and suggested she consider applying, she probably would have rejected the idea. She was not one to seek the advice of parents. Except to cook fish.

So I said nothing. But she saw the article and took action on her own. The next day on her own she went down to Nordstrom's and bought a conservative dark blue power suit, shoes and bag to match. On her mother's credit card, of course. I later asked her why she chose that particular outfit. She said she had gone out to the airport and had observed the flight attendants coming and going, their uniforms, their hairstyles, and their make-up. As a result, she had redone her hair, restyled her make-up to be more conservative and now had an outfit to match the image she wished to project.

The following day she was gone for most of the day, but returned home flushed and excited. She had been to the first interview. There had been literally hundreds of applicants, she said. She was one of about two hundred asked to return for another day of evaluations.

At the end of the next day, she returned home, again flushed with victory. She had been asked to come back for a third day of interviews. She was one of about twenty. At the end of the third day she raced home to tell us that she had been one of a dozen applicants accepted into the TWA flight attendant training program at their training facility in Kansas City and would be leaving within a month, subject only to her physical exam and a drug test.

Several weeks later we saw her off at the airport. The

following weeks were a flurry of telephone calls from Kansas City. Every evening we got a blow-by-blow description of the day's events. The training was structured so that every participant had to receive a passing grade each day in every course, from first-aid, to survival techniques over water, to customer service, to grooming, in order to continue in the training program and to eventually become an employee. Any failure along the way meant being dropped from the program. Allison was determined not to allow that to happen to her. And it didn't.

She graduated from the program and returned home triumphant. Within two weeks she was instructed to report to J. F. Kennedy Airport for duty. Her life and ours would never be the same again. She was barely twenty years old.

Some people are born to fly, born to travel great distances, pass through countless time zones without difficulty, born to live a life in transit. Allison, it turned out, was one of them. A normal schedule for her would be to work a flight back from London, or Paris, or Rome, catch a standby flight across the continent to her home in Portland, have her hair done, spend a day or two with us and her local friends, all envious of her new life style, catch a flight back to New York City, pick up her dry cleaning, catch a flight to The Bahamas for a weekend on the beach at Nassau, and then fly back to New York in time for her next working trip out, to Madrid, or Barcelona, or wherever. And all without a moment of what we know as jet lag. She had turned an important corner in her life and had matured into a lively and interesting world traveler. And had reconnected with her siblings and us. The Sky Girl celebrated her twenty-first birthday in Paris.

She celebrated her twenty-third birthday here at

home. She had been grounded with a minor health issue, an ear infection. While she didn't feel particularly ill, she was not allowed to fly until her doctor released her to do so. As a result she spent her time lounging around the house, chatting, joking, telling us of her experiences in the various countries she traveled to, of the intrigues of her roommates' romances, and of life in New York. It was a sweet time for us all. This was a different Allison. At last.

And then she received her medical clearance and was gone once again, first to be part of the wedding party of one of her flight attendant roommates, in Virginia, and then back to New York to resume working flights. Looking back I have often wondered if that lovely period of time with Allison was meant in some way to be our last Good-Bye. As it turned out, it was.

CHAPTER THREE

AND SO THIS FRIDAY MORNING I SHOWER AND SHAVE WHILE Linnette makes breakfast, and then we switch places, and she showers while I scan the newspaper and sip a cup of coffee. By 7 a.m. she is ready to leave for her commute to school, where she teaches third grade, and I am ready to head to the Multnomah County Courthouse in downtown Portland. I have a routine court appearance, an arraignment. I will make the court appearance before I go out to my law office in East Multnomah County. I have a new client coming in at 10:30 a.m. Since my court appearance is at 9 a.m., I have plenty of time. I can probably stop at the courthouse coffee shop before returning and have another cup of coffee and dabble in some of the local legal gossip with my fellow attorneys, all, like me, toiling in the halls of justice. I am in no rush.

By 10:00 a.m. I am on the freeway heading east toward my office and arrive shortly before 10:30 a.m. My client is already waiting for me. This is a new client, a young man wanting advice on a child custody matter. I greet my secretary, Ann, acknowledge the client, hang up my coat, check my messages and retire to my office to return a couple of telephone calls before I begin my interview with the new client. When I am ready to talk to him, I give Ann my standard instruction not to disturb us while we are in consultation, except from a judge or in an emergency. I usher him into my office, close the door and we begin reviewing his situation.

At about 11 a.m. Ann knocks, opens the door and slips in.

"There's a police officer here to see you," she says.

"What does he want," I ask, unhappy at the interruption.

"I don't know," she answers, "but she says she needs to see you right away."

I get up from my desk, excuse myself and leave the office, closing the door behind me. On the far side of the waiting room, as close to the entrance as she can get, is a Multnomah County Deputy Sheriff, rocking back and forth from one leg to the other. She is clearly nervous. She approaches me tentatively and hands me a business card with her name and official position printed on it. On the back is written another name and a long-distance telephone number.

"You need to call that man," she says almost in a whisper, glancing over at Ann, as if our conversation is meant to be a private one. She points to the business card. "He's a detective in the police department in Secaucus, New Jersey."

"I don't know anybody in Secaucus, New Jersey," I say, a bit frustrated and upset at having been interrupted. I'm thinking I probably have a client who has been picked up on some charge on the East coast. But the police officer turns quickly and is gone out the door without another word. I am left standing there, the card still in my hand. My first inclination is to return to my client and finish our interview and make the call later. But then, for some reason, I decide differently.

I go into an unoccupied office next to mine, close the door and sit for a few moments. Then I dial the telephone. Who could I know in New Jersey, I wonder? I have a nephew who lives in New Jersey, but I can't imagine he would have any reason to contact me in this way. As I am dialing the number a coldness begins to slowly creep over me: *Allison.*

But she's not in New Jersey, I say to myself. She could be anywhere in the world. But not likely New Jersey. A voice answers, and I ask for the detective. My call is transferred. A moment later a man answers. I identify myself. There is a long silence on the line. I feel the coldness spreading further throughout my body. Allison . . .

"Do you have a daughter named Allison Talney?" he asks.

"I do," I say. "Why do you ask?"

"Does she have any identifying marks or scars?" he asks, as impersonally as if he were doing a survey for some commercial product.

"What has happened?" I am suddenly close to screaming.

"There's been an accident here," he says, almost casually.

"Is she hurt?" I ask.

There is another long pause. The sensation of coldness seeps deeper, and I grip the telephone as if it is some sort of lifeline.

"I'm afraid I must tell you she is deceased," he says. "But we need to positively identify her, as the young woman in question had no I.D. on her." He sounds like he's reading from a script. My daughter has suddenly become "the young woman in question."

At this point my mind enters an entirely different place. My voice seems to come from somewhere else. Somehow I answer more questions regarding scars, medical history, physical description and the like.

"We will need you and her mother here in New Jersey to make a final identification." He pauses. "And of course you will need to make arrangements to transport her remains back to Oregon, if that is your intention." He pauses again. "How soon can you get here?" The word "remains" strikes me like a hammer blow. Her remains! Suddenly my daughter is no longer "the young woman in question," but has become "remains." I say something that seems to satisfy the detective, but I don't remember exactly how we end the conversation. I set down the phone receiver. I am suddenly and finally there sitting in that vacant office alone with this terrible news, information no one else here has as yet except me. I have been told my daughter is dead. She has been dead now for hours. While I was shaving, drinking coffee, making court appearances, chatting with friends, and interviewing prospective clients, my daughter lay dead on a slab in a morgue somewhere in New Jersey. And I, her father, did not even know it. Did not, somehow, sense the tragedy unfolding across the continent in the middle of the night. I had blissfully slept through my daughter's final moments. I do not understand how that could possibly be. It is not something I could ever have imagined.

For what seems a long time, I sit there in that empty room in a daze, staring at the blank gray walls, trying to somehow process this information. All the while, my new client sits patiently in my office, waiting for me. Finally Ann comes in to find out what is keeping to me. Somehow I blurt out the news and ask her to inform the young man I will not be available to him and that he will need to seek help elsewhere.

Stunned, Ann hurries out of the office and quietly closes the door. I continue to sit there.

And now I begin to slowly feel a certain numbness, a coldness taking over my body. I do not realize it at the time, but I am learning the first lesson of grief: the growing pain of loss. And not just emotional pain or mental pain, as I might have imagined, but physical pain. The feeling that my chest has suddenly been torn open and my heart quite literally ripped from my body. I have never experienced such agony.

"Allison. Allison."

I speak her name. It seems to echo briefly, but then it quickly disappears, absorbed into the grayness of the cold and silent world that now surrounds me.

CHAPTER FOUR

But now I know somehow I have to act. I'm a father. I can't just sit here. I lift the phone and dial Linnette's school. Jean, the school secretary answers. I tell her that I must to talk with Linnette, that it is an emergency. She is in class and is usually not to be disturbed. Something, however, in the desperate sound of my voice apparently tells Jean otherwise. She doesn't ask me why, but sets the phone down and is gone. I can hear the tapping of her high heels echoing off into the distance. I try to practice what I will say. It is about five minutes before Linnette comes on the line. It seems like an hour. My hastily made preparations disappear instantly with the sound of her voice.

"There has been a terrible accident back east," I blurt out. "Allison is dead."

I know no other way to break the news. I can hear her long wail over the telephone line.

"I'm coming to get you," I say. "Be in front of the school. I'm leaving right now. We are needed in New Jersey."

With no further explanation, I hang up, stop by the office of Bob, the attorney with whom I share office space, quickly tell him what has happened, grab my coat, tell Ann I must leave, and stagger out the door. She is watching me leave. I can see tears glistening in her eyes. I stumble across the parking lot at the back of our office building, climb into my car and pull out into traffic. I am almost blinded by my own tears.

Somehow I make it to the school, which is only about five miles away, in Gresham, a neighboring town. My mind is racing uncontrollably, playing back over and over the words of the detective in New Jersey, his casual voice and calm demeanor. How can the messenger of death be that calm, that casual? That professional? So detached? It doesn't seem right. A young woman is dead. Our lives, in that brief moment, now no more than broken sticks. Somehow he should be screaming and hysterical too.

I make it safely to the school. Linnette is waiting in the parking lot. Jean and several of Linnette's colleagues are standing with her, holding her up. Tears are streaming down her face. Tears are streaming down mine. We load her into the car and they wave good-bye to us. I head for home. Our conversation is a blur. I tell her what has been told to me as best I can. We are both crying. I can barely see the road ahead.

At home we begin immediately to pack bags and prepare to leave, although we have no idea what we are doing. We have made no plans. We are just reacting. Within minutes, however, the telephone rings and it is a representative from TWA offering to help. She has taken the initiative and arranged flights for us, leaving at 2 p.m., if we can be ready and at the Portland airport, arriving in

Newark, New Jersey in the early evening. Grateful for this help, I say of course, we can. It is now about 12:30 p.m. I telephone my sister Lyn and our son-in-law Ben to tell them what has happened and that we're leaving. Linnette telephones her older sister Barbara. We ask them all to carry on for us while we are gone. We are especially concerned for our other children, and our parents. We complete our packing, throwing some clothes into the carry-on bags, and leave for the airport.

There are no TWA flights that fly into Newark, so we have been put on Continental airlines, through Denver, where we are to change planes. When we land in Denver it is snowing, even though it is April. Due to mechanical difficulties as well as the snowstorm, our flight out of Denver to Newark is delayed until after midnight. We pace the endless terminal hallways for all those hours, those long, lonely corridors of colorless floor tile and stark walls. We are unable to sit, unable to eat, unable to sleep, unable to do anything but pace. Linnette paces in one direction, I pace in the other direction. Hour after hour. All the while our minds play back in an endless loop, the news. I feel like I have been driven into a brick wall. And underlying all of it is the hope, the one last desperate hope, that this might really be a mistake. Not our daughter. Surely, God, not ours. I am more than ready to sacrifice someone else's daughter. After all, the police weren't positive. The young woman had no identification on her. It could be someone else.

But in our hearts we know it is not so. While we have never heard of the young man she was with, Allison has lots of boyfriends. All over the world. It is common for her not to bother taking her purse or any I.D. with her, just walk out the door, ready to party. He was a TWA employee. And the description of her was accurate right down to the location of the surgery scar from her appendectomy. And so we continue our vigil and pace. We pace up one corridor, down another, passing each other from time to time like ghosts until at last they call our flight.

We arrive in Newark airport about 6 a.m. on Saturday. For all those hours flying across the country we sit like zombies, staring up at the curved ceiling of the airplane, our faces wet with tears, our minds tortured by fear of what we now face. Periodically, flight attendants stop by offering coffee, water or a blanket. We wave them off. I watch a young flight attendant struggle to push a food cart up and down the narrow aisle and feel a sudden and unexplainable burst of anger. Allison, too, should be just doing her job at this moment. Another young flight attendant, blonde, slender like Allison, her back to me, suddenly turns, sees my stricken face and smiles. I can't respond.

But finally we see the sun rising ahead of us, casting red streaks of light across the early morning skyline, the tall buildings of New York City far off in the distance. The plane slowly circles above Newark for what seems forever, and at last we land. We deplane and drag ourselves into the main area of the terminal, pulling our bags behind us. We see a young, uniformed police officer leaning casually against a pillar closely watching the passengers disembarking. I approach him.

"Are you looking for the Talneys by any chance?" I ask.

He nods and introduces himself. We follow him silently, like whipped puppies, out of the terminal to a waiting police car parked at the curb just outside the main door. He ushers us into the back seat and we begin the drive to Secaucus. Morning traffic is already stacking up on the turnpike. We just sit there unable to converse with him. He makes no effort to converse with us. He is not unkind, he's just doing his job. He pulls into the entrance of a Hilton Hotel and drops us off. He tells us the department will give us a couple of hours to try to rest and get something to eat, and that a car will come to pick us up at the hotel at 9 a.m. He tells us we will need to be interviewed by detectives investigating the accident but that first we must go to the Hudson County Morgue to identify the body. She is now officially "the body." And with that he is gone, the police cruiser sliding back out into the morning traffic. We check in at the front desk and are given a room on one of the upper floors. It has all been arranged in advance by the Secaucus Police Department.

Finally, up in the room we settle in as best we can and decide we need to lie down on one of the two queen-sized beds hoping to sleep for a while. We have had no sleep since Thursday night. I close the thick drapes tightly and darken the room. Neither of us is hungry. It is deathly quiet, except for the occasional sounds of Spanish mixed with English of the room maids and other employees who walk past our door. We lie there motionless and stare up into the dark ceiling, but we can't sleep. We are unable to even speak to one another. There are no words possible at this point. Instead we just lie there in the dark, Linnette desperately clutching my hand, my eyes focused on the bleakness that now seems so absolute.

MAGIC

THE MAGIC SET WAS UNDER THE CHRISTMAS TREE AS requested. Within a short time, wearing her makeshift black cape with the silver sequins spelling out The Amazing Allison, her tall, black magician's hat, and waving her magic wand, she had been transformed. The stairway up to the bedrooms became her stage. We would sit in wonder at the base of the stairs and from the bathroom she would suddenly appear, to thunderous applause, her magic wand in hand, and quickly pull a fake rabbit out of her hat, or find nickels in odd places, like behind her ears, and all the while, distracting us from her awkward hand movements with witty patter she had written herself. At eight years of age, she had fully embraced show business and for several years she performed for us, and all the neighbor kids on demand. Once she got into Jr. High School, however, the social pressures became such that she would no longer put on her act. The magic set went onto the closet floor of her bedroom, along with the tall hat, the wand and the black cape. The Amazing Allison took to teenage rebellion as she had once taken to magic. Yesterday I found the magic set, still stored in its place on the closet floor, just beneath where her pressed airline uniforms are hung. Once again she is The Amazing Allison, appearing and reappearing, as if by magic.

CHAPTER FIVE

It is 9 a.m. We are waiting in the lobby of the hotel. We tried to rest but couldn't, so we finally just come down to the lobby to be in the presence of others. Except for the tears running down our faces, we want to think we look like everybody else. There are business types coming and going. A convention of some sort is taking place on the premises, and men in dark suits and women in formal office attire, all with name tags stuck on their chests, are gathering in groups, talking loudly, and drinking their morning coffee, munching on scones and croissants. We are wearing the same clothes we wore yesterday on the long flight from Portland.

It is a gray, drizzly day. We are staring through the massive plate glass windows out into the parking lot when a police cruiser pulls up to the entrance of the hotel and comes to a stop. It must be here for us. No one else seems to pay any attention to it. We leave the hotel, and a young uniformed Lieutenant gets out of the car and greets us.

Like his predecessor at the airport, he is polite and professional. This cannot be good duty for him. He directs
us into the back seat of the cruiser, and we leave the hotel
grounds, heading from Secaucus back toward the city of
Newark and the site of the Hudson County Morgue.

This is our first opportunity to really get any information about the accident and the state of the investigation.
He tells us where the accident occurred on the New Jersey
Turnpike, just within the city limits of Secaucus. Not far,
in fact, from our hotel. Just three blocks away. It is difficult to comprehend that we are now just within blocks of
where our daughter died in the rain and the dark, alone
and without us. We can see the long stretch of concrete
from the car as we speed past the entrance ramps, down
onto the turnpike itself.

We inquire about the young man who was driving and
are told that he is apparently still in intensive care and
may or may not survive. He had received massive head
injuries. His future, if he does live, is very much in doubt.
We are told he is hospitalized just a short distance away.
We can see the hospital from the car as we pass by. The
Lieutenant points it out to us. I can imagine the young
man's parents and family waiting agonized outside the
operating room or intensive care unit. Part of me says
they are lucky to have hope. And part of me says that if
what happened had to happen, we are better off to know
that our daughter is now safe in death. Nothing more can
harm her ever again.

The Hudson County Morgue is a nondescript-looking
government building. We pull into the parking lot and get
out. Linnette and I can hardly walk. We hang onto each
other like novice ice skaters struggling to keep upright,

struggling to keep from falling down. We weave and reel across the open space of the parking lot to the front door. The young Lieutenant walks with us and holds open the wide, double doors. We stumble into the lobby. The reality of having to now identify what remains of our daughter has hit us full force. It is incomprehensible. We have no idea what to expect. In a daze we enter the offices of the Medical Examiner. There is a strong chemical smell, like a hospital. We are met by a large, bearded man in a long, white coat. He introduces himself. He is the Chief Medical Examiner. He is kind but forceful.

"This must be done," he says, his tone suggesting he understands how difficult it must be, but he gives us no choice. He ushers us into a large room and seats us at a long conference table. He carefully takes a slim manila envelope from his inside coat pocket and spreads its contents out on the table. "These are the items taken from the body or found near the body," he tells us. "Do you recognize any of them?"

Through tears we both nod dumbly. There is the emerald ring we gave Allison just three weeks ago for her twenty-third birthday, badly twisted out of shape. Another ring, also badly twisted, that I had given her a year or two before is also there. A delicate, silver necklace. A small silver rose, like a single charm that we have never seen before. Some coins. Nothing more.

We no longer have any illusions about what or whom we will see once we enter the next room, the viewing room. Any desperate hope we may have had that this loss might somehow pass to someone else is gone. The medical examiner carefully puts the items back in the envelope and hands it to Linnette. It is a small act of finality, a transaction that seals our grief in place. We stand up, supporting ourselves with the table, Linnette clutching the last few fragments of our daughter's life in her hands.

"It is time," he tells us gently, moving us toward the viewing room. This room is small and sparsely furnished, containing only several straight-backed chairs. The lights are dimmed. We sit down, the police officer beside us as a witness to observe what transpires. We move only when and where we are told to move. We do what we are told to do. In the viewing room, attached high on the far wall, like in a hospital room, is suspended a large television monitor. The medical examiner tells us to watch the screen and they will tell us when the image of the body is about to be revealed. We stare at the screen. A few moments pass. We continue to stare. We can then hear the click of the monitor being turned on. A flash of light appears in the center of the screen and then disappears.

"Now," a voice calls out from a loudspeaker located somewhere above us in the darkness. The blank black screen slowly brightens. At last the vague, distorted image of a human face and upper torso comes into view. Gradually the image sharpens. The battered, beaten face we see is Allison's face. There is no doubt. We need see no more. We both turn away. The wail that instinctively emanates from us in unison is proof enough. Together we turn back and the image of Allison then slowly fades into darkness and is gone.

With the police officer guiding us we stumble across the parking lot to the car. We sit motionless in the back seat of the police cruiser, the image we have just seen running constantly across our minds like a recurring nightmare. A nightmare in broad daylight. I look at

Linnette and she looks back at me, her face streaked and pale. We can only sit there in silence as the graying landscape of Secaucus comes back into view. We have just looked into the reality that will now dominate our lives. We have become witnesses to our own future.

We next must be interviewed by an investigator from the Secaucus Police Department. We enter the building that houses the Department where we are met by the detectives handling the case. We sit in an interviewing room and stare blankly at blank walls, painted institutional green, while the detectives sit across from us at the institutional green metal conference table and take notes of our conversation. What appear to be police reports of the accident lie in a small heap on the table, but I don't think to ask for copies. At this point, I can't imagine wanting a copy. Sitting there turned away from us we can see large, 8" X 10" photos of what must be the accident scene. I can see one on top of the pile that shows what appears to be a sports car upended, lying across the roadway. Black and white photos, glossy and grim. After this meeting we are told we will be free to make arrangements to return home with Allison. We are grateful when the detective calls her by her name: Allison. All in all, the officers are professional and kind.

At the police station the interview is brief. They say they have no reason to believe there has been any intentional criminal activity involved. They inquire about such matters as life insurance coverage, beneficiaries and the like. They inquire about anything that might establish or suggest any kind of motive to cause a fatal accident. There were no skid marks at the accident scene. There was no known mechanical problem with the car. There was no evidence that alcohol or drugs were involved. The supposition is that the young man, now known to us as James Kiefner of Brooklyn, New York, may simply have fallen asleep at the wheel and by the time he awoke and realized what was happening, it was too late. The car was out of control. The perils of driving too far and staying at the wheel too long. A foolish misjudgment. An accident waiting to happen. We answer the questions as best we can, still in a state of extreme agitation from our experience at the Medical Examiner's office.

Then we are returned to our hotel. On the way we sit silently in the back seat of the police cruiser. The Lieutenant makes no effort to engage us in further conversation. What is there to say? He pulls into the parking lot of the hotel and drops us off at the front door. He smiles and wishes us well. He waves as he circles the parking lot and turns out into traffic. We will not see him again. There are now more arrangements to be made. The Department will keep us informed of any further developments in the investigation. Assuming he lives, it is possible Mr. Kiefner could be charged with some major traffic violation or a crime such as manslaughter, but that has not been determined as yet. It is all very professional and factual. A file is being created. A judgment will be made.

It is now about noon. We go back up to our room. The drapes are still drawn and the room is as dark as when we left it. The room maid has been in to clean, but there was little for her to do. It occurs to me that I did not even think to leave a tip for her. One bed was left unused. The other still has the bedspread on it with just the imprint of our bodies to show we have been here. We had showered this morning and used some of the towels. Otherwise, the room was undisturbed.

Exhausted, we again lie down on one of the beds hoping to finally fall asleep. It is early Saturday afternoon. We have had no sleep since Thursday night. But the image we have seen in the Medical Examiner's office continues to drift back and forth across the darkened ceiling above us, a ghostly presence that I know will be part of our lives forever. Still unable to sleep, we just lie there stiff and motionless, silent, holding hands and staring upwards, into the floating death mask that is the face of our daughter, bruised and swollen.

CHAPTER SIX

We have tried to rest but can't. Finally we just get up and I open the drapes. It is still early afternoon, a cloudy gray and overcast sort of day, a drizzly rain. From the room we can see the Turnpike where the accident occurred off in the distance. We can also see the hospital building where James Kiefner lies in intensive care. We feel a sudden desire to make contact with the hospital and try to learn the status of the young man, if possible. We talk it over and decide we want the family to know that we too are concerned for his survival and that we hope he is doing as well as possible under the circumstances.

I search the dresser for the phone book and look up the telephone number of the hospital and call, asking for the intensive care unit. A nurse answers and I ask how the young man is doing. She doesn't reveal any information other than to say that he is still in surgery. Then unexpectedly she asks if I would like to speak with his mother. Somewhat surprised by the offer, I say I would and the line goes quiet for several minutes. Now that I'm faced with the prospect of actually speaking with a family member, I'm not sure what I can possibly say.

Then the phone is picked up and a woman's voice says "Hello." Her voice is shaky and uncertain. I tell her who I am, that we are here in New Jersey and that Linnette and I are inquiring about her son's condition. I need say no more. Once she realizes who I am, she immediately becomes defensive and begins explaining that her son was not at fault and that she is convinced he must have been run off the road by another car. She apparently assumes we are just attempting to lay blame. I can now understand how she might think that. I try to calm her down, but she is in no condition to listen. I realize it was a mistake to have contacted her. Finally I just give her our address and telephone number in Portland and ask her to let us know how he is recovering. She makes no effort to record the information or to inquire about Allison or our arrangements for her. I wish her well and we terminate the conversation. This is our first, and as it turns out, our last and only direct contact with or from anyone in the Kiefner family.

But at least now we have actually been able to do something. What we must do now is to make arrangements to take Allison home. We have no idea what to do or how to go about it. Despite the confusion, despair and exhaustion of the moment, however, we somehow still find within ourselves the strength and will to be a mother and father to Allison even in death. Our immediate goal is to bring her home and as quickly as possible. That now becomes our focus. But we are strangers here. We have had no preparation for what we must do now.

I look in the yellow pages of the telephone book for a

funeral director and locate a mortuary that appears to be reasonably close to the hotel. Mack Memorial Home. It is a Saturday and I don't even know if there would be anyone there to receive our call. I telephone and the owner Henry Mack himself answers. In desperation I try as best I can to explain what has happened and what we need to accomplish. He responds with a calm authority that suggests he has dealt with situations like ours many times before. Because it is a weekend, he tells me it will not be possible to have Allison ready for a return to Portland today. He says he will arrange to pick her up at the office of the Medical Examiner in Newark, take her to his establishment, prepare her for travel, and that she can be ready for the afternoon flight back to Portland tomorrow, Sunday.

At no time does he refer to her as the "remains" or the "body." He calls her by her name. I am grateful for that. He agrees that he will pick us up at the hotel late tomorrow morning, along with Allison, and take us all to Kennedy Airport, which is over fifty miles away from Secaucus. He also offers to come to the hotel now and take us back to the funeral home to meet with him. It is the kindness of a man whose business is grief. We could not have met a person more ready to address the immediate needs of a family in distress than Henry Mack.

Soon he arrives, driving a somber, black Buick Roadmaster four-door sedan. We are waiting for him in the lobby. Mr. Mack is an older man, gray haired and dressed in a dark suit and tie, a mortician's uniform. He drives us the short distance to his business establishment. A funeral is ending just as we arrive. People in their Sunday best are milling around as a funeral procession is being formed in the parking lot, cars lining up, motorcycles of off-duty police officers providing escort revving up. It is a brief glimpse into our own unfolding future.

We meet with Mr. Mack in his office. He discusses his services and the logistics. We make the necessary arrangements, sign a promissory note and contract for his services, and obtain information on how to secure assistance at the other end of the flight. We had been in such a panic to leave Portland we don't even have a checkbook with us for any of these expenses, or even a small retainer. Mr. Mack agrees without hesitation to provide his services solely on our promise to pay him after we have returned home. His trust in us is a lesson in humanity for which we will always be grateful.

Mr. Mack has also cut out an article from the local newspaper about the accident. We had not seen it. It has the usual dispassionate, disconnected tone of a news report. We both notice immediately, however, that the headline refers to Allison as a "Stewardess," an occupational title she would have despised. She was a "flight attendant," not a "stewardess," and was quick to correct anyone who said otherwise. I look at Linnette and she looks at me. Despite all that has happened, we both have to smile.

But then we read the substance of the report and our smiles quickly disappear. We read that the reporter had attempted to contact the Kiefner family for a comment on the accident and was told by a relative, who refused to be identified, that the family "didn't care to deal too much with outsiders." That certainly proved to be the case.

Mr. Mack returns us to the hotel. It is now mid-afternoon. We have not eaten since breakfast the day before. We have not slept since Thursday night. I close the drapes again and we order some food from room service and again lie down, hoping to sleep. It is still impossible, even within the darkened room. Room service arrives, and we set the trays on the small, round dining table in the corner, and we just sit at the table and look down at the covered plates. I lift off the covers, but the sandwiches remain on the trays uneaten, the coffee carafe cools. We cannot bring ourselves to even eat.

Suddenly the telephone rings, and the first of many calls from one end of the continent to the other begin. It is our daughter, Jennifer, and our son, Aaron. We are grateful to know they are finally together. He has come down from Seattle and the two of them are holding each other up. We long to be with them but are torn by our need to stay with Allison and to see her home. Jennifer tells us that she spoke with Linnette's mother, Nancy, by phone and was the one to have to tell her that her granddaughter had been killed. It was very difficult for both of them. However, Jennifer is a social worker, by training and by disposition. Even as a child, she was always taking care of others. And now she was taking care of her grandmother.

"Grandmom was devastated," she tells us. "But Granddad is too far gone to understand what has happened." Al has been slipping quietly into Alzheimer's for several years.

Linnette's older sister, Barbara, was with their parents, Nancy and Al, when Jennifer called but she hadn't yet told them of the death. We talk to Aaron too, but he is quiet and pulled down deep into himself. He doesn't have much to say, but we know by his silence that he is suffering. We long to be with them but are torn and know our present need is to be here. It is good to talk with them both, however, and to know they are there to support each other, along with our son-in-law, Ben.

I think how only last summer I worried so much about Aaron, who is now in ROTC training at the University of Washington, then in airborne school down at Fort Benning, Georgia, and knowing that he was nightly bailing out of airplanes with a heavy pack on his back, and how dangerous it was. In my dreams I would see his body hurtling and twisting down through the humid night air while I waited beneath him anxious for his chute to finally open and for him to be safe on the ground again. Once we let them go, we no longer have even an illusion of control over their lives or what happens to them. Later we also talk to my brother and sister-in-law in Canada, and my sister and brother-in-law in Portland. It does us good to have these contacts and to know that we are not entirely alone in this strange hotel in this strange and, for us, a foreign city.

Unable to eat and unable to sleep, late in the afternoon, toward dusk, we decide we must get out of the room, get some fresh air and just walk. There is now nothing more to do here to get Allison home. I had obtained information on a funeral home in Portland, near our home, The Little Chapel of the Chimes, and they have agreed to pick Allison up at the airport when she arrives and transport her to their funeral home. We will meet with them when we return. Consequently, we have now done everything that we can do or needs to be done here and we now have only time on our hands.

We leave the hotel and walk down the street as evening falls, past the hospital, and find ourselves in a city park along the banks of the Hudson River. It is cold and a misty rain is still falling. I shiver from more than just the cold as we stand on a point of land, looking out across the water. We can see the lights of Newark in the distance. We are alone in the park. There is no one else around. On the other side of the park there is a playground with swings and slides, and beyond that, tennis courts. All are deserted. The swings sway and clank with a slight wind off the water. To me this is an alien landscape, made bleaker by the events that have brought us here. My only wish is to take our daughter and leave this place that has meant so much sorrow, this place that has now become the scene of so much that has been destroyed in our lives, so much that was to be her future and ours.

Ships of varying sizes slowly pass on their way either into port or out of the harbor toward open water, their running lights twinkling like low lying stars in the descending darkness. We watch silently as a huge container ship slides past, heading out to sea, its crew-members and a few passengers lining the decks along the railings of the ship, waving, perhaps to us. They seem to be saying, Good-bye, Good-bye to what might be the last of land they'll see for many days, their final destinations quite possibly unknown.

CHAPTER SEVEN

IT IS LATE SATURDAY EVENING. THE DRAPES ARE STILL DRAWN AND our hotel room is pitch-black. We again lie down on one of the beds together, staring up into the darkness like wounded animals. How long we lie there like that I don't know. It seems like hours. We are trying to sleep. But I can't.

My mind continues to race. It is like an endless loop of audio and videotape playing and replaying the events of the past thirty-six hours. It is as if I am being informed over and over again of Allison's death. Over and over. I hear the voices of police officers, medical examiners, nameless others. I see my daughter's beaten face, etched into the dark space that is now my mind. I lie quietly, holding myself motionless. But inside I am not quiet, I am not still. Inside I am screaming for relief.

Linnette lies beside me on her stomach, her face pushed down into the pillow. In time I sense that she may actually have fallen asleep. Her breathing takes on a regularity and her body seems to relax ever so slightly. Afraid

that my restlessness will waken her I slowly lift myself
from the bed and feel my way in the dark to the small
dining table in the far corner of the room. The air-conditioning is working overtime and there is a chill in the air,
so I quickly wrap myself in a bedspread taken from the
other bed and sit down at the table. I sit there just staring
down at the dim outline of the tray of stale sandwiches
and cold coffee.

Slowly, however, little by little, I begin to sense a
change coming over me. I become aware that I am slowly
filling up, inflating it seems, with air. It is a strange sensation. It is like nothing I have ever experienced before.
It is not unpleasant, but at the same time it is somewhat
frightening. I find myself concentrating, despite the noise
of the horrific details that continue to play in my mind,
on the blackness that now envelopes me. I feel myself
expanding. At the same time, I sense a tension, an energy
in the room that I can't identify or name. I am no longer
alone. It is an inexplicable experience, entirely beyond my
rational world. And finally, with the sense that I have been
invaded by an outside force, a message appears across my
darkened mind, as on an inner screen:

"It's okay. I'm all right."

I immediately recognize the cadence, the tone, and
rhythm of Allison's voice. It is exactly what she would say
and how she would say it. It is what she said to us so many
times from so many places in the world. "It's okay. I'm
all right." I sit there stunned. The message holds for what
must be twenty to thirty seconds, an eternity, and then
begins to slowly fade away, to disintegrate, to dissolve back
into the dark air. At the same time I feel myself begin to
gradually deflate, like an inner tube with a slow leak losing

its air. And then suddenly there is a final rush of energy, almost a whirling sound, like a small cyclone that seems to be swirling around me and around the room and then is gone. Whatever or whoever was there is there no longer. And I sense will not ever return. One final moment.

I sit there in the dark stunned and utterly depleted. I am weak and strangely at peace. I continue to sit in the chair but I don't know for how long. It could be minutes or hours. But at last I stand up and move to the empty bed and lie down, covering myself with the bedspread, as I am suddenly feeling the chill of the air-conditioning again. Instantly it seems, I fall into a deep sleep and I sleep soundly and dreamlessly until morning. I wake to the sunrise with a quiet calmness. I feel the first sense of relief since the Deputy Sheriff came to my office in Portland, the bearer of such terrible news. And I am left to wonder, and will for the rest of my life, just what has happened to me.

What this experience was, I don't know. But even years later as I record this event, I cannot explain it. I am a lawyer by training. I look for evidence to prove events, not hearsay, not tarot cards, not psychics. But now I only know what happened and how it affected me. I feel that out of this terrible loss I have nonetheless been the beneficiary of an extraordinary gift. I sense that the power of love, somehow and in some profound way has conquered the laws of nature. In that dark room I met face to face with that which cannot be explained. And cannot be ignored or disregarded.

"It's okay. I'm all right."

CHAPTER EIGHT

THE NEXT MORNING I DO NOT TELL LINNETTE ABOUT MY EXPE-
rience for fear she will not believe me and think that I
have lost my mind. Or in the alternative, will wonder why
she was not the beneficiary too of such a visitation, or
such an experience.

It is Sunday, our travel day, and Mr. Mack will be
picking us up about 11 a.m. for our trip to Kennedy Airport. We must have Allison's body at the TWA shipping
terminal by 2 p.m. and our flight leaves the main terminal
at 4:30 p.m. We still have not eaten anything since Friday
morning, and I know we must try to eat something. I
know too that we need to get out of the room and see
and be with other human beings still able to go about the
routine business of their daily lives.

We sit in the hotel restaurant playing with our food,
scrambled eggs and toast, but neither of us has much of an
appetite. But we try to eat. All around us other guests are
enjoying the hotel Sunday all-you-can-eat brunch, with huge

plates of food from the buffet, champagne and fancy drinks. We toy with our eggs and toast and drink some coffee.

At 11 a.m. sharp a long, black hearse pulls into the parking lot of the hotel and parks beneath the entrance canopy. We have already checked out and are waiting just outside the double doors with our bags. We walk over to the waiting hearse and Mr. Mack, still dressed in somber black, takes our bags from us, like a mortician turned bellhop. We look into the back of the hearse and can see through the side windows, past the maroon, velvet curtains, the long, cardboard carton that contains our daughter. She is packed for shipping. We are both immediately struck by the irony of the sky girl who flew for a living, who passed through time zones without giving it a thought, will now be cargo to be stowed in the hold of an airplane. A human life now encased in cardboard and wrapped tightly with duct tape.

Mr. Mack drives through the center of Manhattan on his way to JFK. Despite the fact that it is Sunday morning, the going is slow. The traffic is heavy. I have the sense that we are the lead float in a final parade honoring Allison, driving down the city's main streets, a city where she had enjoyed herself so much. The Great White Way. The Star of Broadway. It is like a final farewell. I almost feel a need to wave to the people rushing along the sidewalks and crossing the street in front of us, as if they too, like the ship's passengers, might suddenly stop, turn and wave back, perhaps calling out, "Good-bye, good-bye." But they're bustling New Yorkers, and they manage to ignore us.

At last we see the outline of the airport coming into view and we approach the shipping terminal for TWA. Mr. Mack drives into the parking lot and backs the hearse as close to the loading dock as he can. He swings open the rear door of the hearse and I step forward to help him carry Allison's body into the terminal. He stops me.

"No. I'll get help from the crew." He holds up his hand.

"I want to help carry her," I insist. "I carried her home from the hospital when she was born." I step past him and reach into the open rear of the hearse. "I need to help carry her now." He nods and does not challenge me further.

Together we lift her from the hearse's bed and, with me on one side and Mr. Mack on the other, we carry her up the steps to the loading dock and into the terminal. She is amazingly light. A crew of several warehousemen are busy getting freight ready for shipment. We are instructed to set her temporary casket down on the scales to be weighed. I look around. There are other packing crates waiting to be loaded onto their respective flights. Refrigerators. Stoves. Heavy equipment of various kinds. And now here is a human being too. My daughter. We gently place her on a conveyer belt, while somewhere off in the distance a motor begins to rumble and she slowly moves away from me, through the dingy flaps of a heavy, plastic curtain into the inner depths of the warehouse, and that is the last I will see of her container until it is safely delivered in Portland.

Linnette has remained in the hearse. I return with tears running down my face. I am remembering how, when we flew to Spain the year before and Allison was part of the flight crew that served us, we watched her doing her job, calming nervous children, serving drinks and food, taking care of her charges on the long flight. How excited she was to be performing for us. And now here she will be residing in the coldness of a cargo hold of possibly one of the very same airplanes she had previously flown in as a crewmember. The irony seems overwhelming to me.

Mr. Mack drives us to the main terminal and lets us out. We thank him profusely for his help and his kindness. He waves and is gone, the black hearse, now empty of all of its passengers, both living and dead, edging its way from the curb and back into traffic.

Inside the terminal, we are immediately approached by a TWA representative. She must recognize us for the tears and long faces. She has our tickets and takes us to a private lounge area where we will not be made to feel like we are in the public eye. There we meet several of Allison's roommates, all of whom are TWA flight attendants. We have met several of them before and of course have heard all about them, their loves, their losses, and their dreams. One of them, Eileen, just got married and Allison was a member of the wedding party in Virginia only two weeks ago. They hug us and sob along with us. We break down again at the sight of them.

It is now about 3 p.m. and our flight will not leave for another hour and a half. They insist on sitting with us while we wait. We spend our time trading Allison stories. There are dozens of them. Many we had not heard before. They tell us how Allison could charm even the French, both with her facility to pick up languages and her utter lack of pretense. Once she was working a charter flight of Jewish travelers from New York taking a trip to Israel. By the time the plane landed in Tel Aviv they all wanted to adopt her. The only people she couldn't charm were the security guards who processed the passengers before they could deplane. She once told me she didn't even dare smile at them, let alone tell them a joke. And so we heard of her continuing love of crazy, outrageous fashions, her often dry and salty humor, her desire to have the highest spike high heels made, her insatiable need for sequins, and their accounts of her boyfriends from various countries around the world. Tomas in Sweden. Marcos in Barcelona.

Finally our flight is called and we board for home. We get hugs and say our good-byes. This is a TWA flight and the members of the flight crew know who we are and why we are traveling. They no doubt also know who our travel companion is. Many of them may very well have worked with her from time to time. Or met her "deadheading" to Portland or back to New York. They have put us in first class to give us as much privacy as the plane will allow. Linnette closes the window shade, and I turn off the ceiling lights to make our area as dark as possible. We both immediately order gin and tonics and sit back. We are still in tears. It doesn't take much to set us off again. As the plane takes off and begins to gain altitude I, tearfully, and now with two or three gin and tonics in me, tell Linnette of my experience during the night before and the message I received.

She doesn't seem to think I'm crazy even as I wonder aloud that I might be. I cannot get it out of my mind who and what is beneath us in the unheated storage hold of the airplane. There is nothing to be done about it. Passengers walk past us on their way to and from the rest rooms, oblivious to our pain. Food service carts rattle up and down the aisles. The passengers to the right of us fall asleep and snore loudly. The movie starts. But we just sit there in the dark and drink until the pain loses its grip on us.

THE AMAZING ALLISON

WE ARE ON A FLIGHT TO SPAIN. SOMEWHERE OVER the Atlantic at 35,000 feet. New York to Madrid. We had intended a flight to Lisbon but it was full and, flying standby, we could not board. So rather than wait two more days for the next flight out to Portugal, we boarded this flight to Madrid and will hop a TAP airline to Lisbon and hopefully catch up with our luggage. The upside of this flight is that Allison is part of the flight crew serving us. We have never seen her at work before. It is amazing to watch her moving about the cabin in her sharply pressed uniform, performing her tasks with such ease and dexterity. Last week she celebrated her twenty-first birthday on a layover in Paris and the crew took her nightclubbing to the Moulin Rouge. Two days ago she was in Tel Aviv, working a charter flight. In between she spent two days and nights in Nassau on the beach getting an early tan. Last night she showed us New York City. We walked down Broadway expecting to run into Robert Goulet. But today the performer is The Amazing Allison. Perhaps she'll find a nickel behind my ear.

CHAPTER NINE

Now that we are home, I have the sense of being grounded once again. At the same time the sense of loss is all the more intense as I realize our return home is a return to the real world. The house is still the same house. The rooms are still the same rooms. The furnishings the same. There are familiar pictures on the walls. Reminders everywhere of what we no longer have. In particular there is Allison's bedroom next to our own. Her possessions are spread casually everywhere, just as she left them only days before.

It is now Monday morning. I contact the TWA shipping terminal at PDX and determine that Allison's body has been picked up by the funeral directors and is now safely in their care. We are relieved to know that she is not still lying somewhere in a cold, impersonal warehouse like so much industrial equipment waiting to be claimed. I make arrangements for us to go to the mortuary and to begin the process of planning a funeral and burial. These are the mundane obligations that temporarily keep us sane. I no longer have any sense of what our lives were like only a few days before.

Telephone calls are coming in from Allison's friends. Local friends are just learning what has happened, and they are in shock. Her best friend lives across the street. Suzanne. The two of them had been friends since we first moved into the neighborhood fifteen years ago, in 1973, when Allison was eight years old. Suzanne is the same age. As we were moving in, Suzanne was at the door, wanting to know if we had any children her age. One of her older sisters, Annette, was soliciting babysitting jobs. Suzanne and Allison hit it off immediately and remained like sisters to the end. It was Suzanne's family she moved in with when as a teenager she decided she couldn't tolerate our house rules. Suzanne's mother was Allison's second mother. When Allison moved to New York to work for TWA, Suzanne also moved there and worked for a time as a nanny. She is overwhelmed. Other friends are checking in. One girlfriend is too shaken to call, and her father calls. They have seen the death notice in the newspaper, and he calls to find out if it is true. I assure him that, sadly, it is. I can hear Allison's friend break into sobs in the background.

The most difficult telephone calls are coming from friends who live elsewhere, many in foreign countries, friends she has made during her world travels, who do not even know of her death and are simply calling in hopes that she might happen to be in Portland, and they ask to talk with her. We get calls from Tomas in Sweden, and Marcos in Barcelona. We must, as patiently as possible, tell each caller that Allison has died. Over and over. There is no easy way to give out that information. Each phone call brings a new round of weeping. On both ends of the line.

In addition, relatives and friends come by. Neighbors bring food. Teacher friends of Linnette's come by to sit with us. Some are people we don't even know very well. They step forward. In the midst of the chaos we are grateful for any show of support.

It is especially hard to give the news to the grandparents. Jennifer told Linnette's mother while we were in New Jersey. My sister told my parents then as well. All were devastated. My mother has suffered from short-term memory loss and dementia for some time and processes the information poorly. My father understands the loss and is heartbroken. Linnette's father has already lost much of his memory to Alzheimer's disease and does not fully comprehend what has happened, and may not even really know who Allison is, but Linnette's mother understands and moans that it should have been her and not one so young. We all understand that sentiment. The unfairness of a young life taken is with us every minute of every day.

Later Linnette and I go to the funeral home to complete arrangements and to visit with Allison. We meet with the staff and plan a time for the funeral. Next we go into the show room filled with caskets and select a suitable one, light blue with pale blue silk lining. Once again we move about as in a nightmare. A terrible nightmare. It has some of the characteristics of buying a new car. "Yes, we'll take that one. Yes, we like that color. No, that lining isn't the right material. No, we won't need that service. Yes, flowers can go there." Even in death there is small talk. We have an intense need to have everything just right. Yet another lesson in grief: the details keep us sane.

This is the first time we have seen Allison since the

awful viewing at the county morgue in Newark. Mr. Mack, and now the morticians at The Little Chapel of the Chimes have had an opportunity to work with her. They have covered most of the bruising and apparent injuries and, even in death she now looks lovely to us. While this picture of her will never entirely replace the one we viewed in New Jersey, it helps. We sit alone in the visitation room and spend some quiet time with her, just talking and looking at her. During the coming days we will spend more time with her. How quickly we overcome our fear of being with the dead. This is still our child.

It is difficult to separate the days between now and the funeral, which is to be held on April 14th. We meet with the minister who will handle the service. Leo Tautfest is the associate pastor at Savage Memorial Presbyterian Church. We are not members of his church, but he and I have known each other through volunteer work. Not being active members of any church, he was an easy choice to officiate the ceremony. He is a younger man, a father himself, and very empathetic. He establishes a rapport with the entire family immediately, as we all meet to discuss the service and to talk about Allison. We tell him some of the many Allison stories that have become legend in our family. We weave them together through our laughter and tears. The parties, the outrageous clothes, the quirky, dry sense of humor. We even talk about her difficult teenage years, the times when we were not so close with her, when she was in rebellion. And also of the reconciliation and her emerging maturity, now cut so short.

We decide we will have a public service so that Allison's friends can attend, and that, in addition to Leo's presiding over the service, it will include our friend, Jim Fleming, who will read several of my poems which were written for Allison. Music will be provided by Owen Smith, a local classical guitarist with whom I have studied. Following the service and a reception at the funeral home there will be a graveside service at Sunset Memorial Gardens where we have purchased gravesites, one for Allison and one on each side of her for Linnette and me. Linnette's parents also purchase plots next to ours for themselves and for Linnette's disabled younger sister, Glenda.

The remaining days until the funeral are now spent at the mortuary with Allison. While we are still in shock, we have little time to dwell on our loss. We visit the funeral home daily and leave gifts of small intimate items to put into the casket with Allison. We spend time just sitting with her, quietly watching over her. Already she is beginning to fade away. We can see tiny physiological changes in her features as death settles in, and she begins her return to the elements. It is difficult for us to see, to trace the intricate disintegration of her body. But it becomes part of our new world, our continuing introduction to the lessons of grief.

DREAMS

And so you dream of death, and in your dream you hold her loss in your hands. You turn it first one way and then the other. It is always the same. Death never changes. But then you waken, the air still with her leaving, the room still dying around you, terminal and strong.

CHAPTER TEN

It is April 14th. The day set for Allison's funeral and burial. We are alone at the house, just Linnette and me and Aaron, who has not yet returned to the university. Jennifer is at her home with her husband, Ben. We will all meet later at the mortuary for a final viewing. The services are set for 1 p.m. We spend the morning getting ready. I am standing before my tie rack trying to pick out a tie to wear. Should it be the red one with the blue stripes? Should it be the solid gray? Suddenly I burst into tears. "God-damn it to Hell!" The thought that I am engrossed in selecting a tie to wear to my daughter's funeral overwhelms me. Finally I just grab a tie and put it around my neck. Something inside me wants to honor Allison by appearing to be whole and intact. And something inside me says this is all so trivial. At this moment I am what I am. Just a sobbing, bereaved father.

Linnette is in the bathroom trying to prepare herself too. We have learned that it is okay to be emotional, even in public. After all, we both cried ourselves across the breadth of the country twice in a commercial airplane. But today we want to make our stand in the presence of family and friends. We do not want to dissolve.

By late morning we go to the mortuary for our one last visit with Allison before the coffin is finally closed and the services begin. We gather in the visiting room, circled around the open casket, the small tokens of love that we have left during the preceding days tucked in beside her. Aaron's army airborne medal. A copy of my first book of poems.

Finally the moment comes when the guests have gathered, and the service is to begin. We say our last goodbye and the mortician slowly closes the lid. We will see her no more. The coffin is wheeled into the chapel and placed at the front by the altar. We take our places in the family section, which we have asked be opened so we can feel part of the community of folks there to pay tribute to our daughter. We do not want to be excluded or isolated now.

Owen Smith, the guitarist, begins playing Bach Preludes. The crowded chapel quiets down. There are sobs coming from various sections of the room. People are seated out into the hallways. Allison's friends are here from all across the country. Our family members are here. My brother and sister-in-law from Canada. Linnette's sister and her sister's husband. My sister and brother-in-law. Our parents. Friends and neighbors. All gathered to support us and to remember Allison.

Leo Tautfest begins the service, telling some of the stories we had discussed with him, at least those that can be told in public. Despite the tears and sobs, there is laughter too, which honors Allison, the party girl, the Sky Girl, the girl who loved sequins and stiletto heels, who collected boyfriends from around the world. He might not be "Mr. Right," but he could be "Mr. Right for the summer," she used to tell us. Now he will always be Mr. Right for the summer. The girl my sister used to call the Butterfly Girl. Jim Fleming reads several of my poems written for Allison when she was born. Owen Smith plays again. And finally it is over.

A reception is held in a room next to the chapel. There is punch, coffee, tea and cookies. The usual fare. Everyone is offering condolences. We are amazingly in control of ourselves. We are the hosts at this gathering in Allison's honor and we pull ourselves together. My mind has gone into neutral for the occasion. I smile. I shake hands. I acknowledge people whose names I cannot recall. I welcome everyone. Linnette looks lovely. She glows with an incandescence that belies the grief that is locked inside. She moves from guest to guest, accepting hugs, their words of condolence, and their individual recollections of Allison.

Finally it is time to go to the cemetery. We assemble the pallbearers, who include Aaron, me, Eric Sabo, a nephew, my brother-in-law, Paul Hybertsen, Paul Peyralans, who is the brother of Suzanne and one of Allison's special friends, and Thor Sabo, Linnette's sister's husband. We carry the closed casket to the waiting hearse backed up to the double doors of the funeral home. I am mindful of the last time I carried her body from the hearse to the terminal in New York City. The casket is not nearly as light as was the shipping carton she traveled in across the country. Cars in the parking lot are filling with people joining in the procession to the cemetery. Off-duty police officers are starting up their motorcycles, ready to supervise what will be a lengthy procession of cars from East Multnomah County to the Sunset Hills Memorial Gardens in the west hills of Portland. It is now mid-afternoon, a weekday, and traffic will already be backing up on the inbound freeway.

The immediate family is driven by employees of the mortuary, immediately behind the hearse. I think of our lonely ride through Manhattan only five days earlier, Mr. Mack driving, with Allison in the back, on our way to JFK airport. This has been such a long and tortured journey in such a short time. And in so many ways, physically and emotionally. We take the Banfield Freeway, I-84 into and through Portland, cross the Willamette River, then head west toward Sunset Hills Memorial Gardens. We enter though the long Vista Ridge tunnel that divides downtown Portland from the west hills. There, suddenly before us, as we maneuver a curve in the roadway, scrawled in huge block letters across the arced side of the tunnel wall someone has written "Allison, We Love You!" We don't know who did that and will probably never know. We are momentarily stunned. It is a shock to see it.

Soon the long procession slowly circles up the hill to the upper parking area of the Memorial Park and we pallbearers carefully carry the casket down the hillside to the gravesite now covered by an awning. The grave lies open and gaping, like a raw wound in the earth, a pile of fresh dirt and sod off to one side. The wide tracks of the heavy equipment that dug the hole are still imprinted into the grass. There is a light rain falling. Everyone gathers around, trying to get under the canopy. Umbrellas are popping open. I help my parents down from the car while

Linnette does the same for her parents. Finally we are all assembled. The graveside service is blessedly brief. Leo offers a few words of commitment and we watch as the casket is slowly lowered into the ground. Flowers from the mortuary have also been brought up and have now been set out around the open grave. With the final Amen, we all stumble back up the hill, past all the other graves and their markers, to the waiting cars and are eventually returned to the mortuary. We ride back in silence. The Sky Girl has been grounded.

Through it all we have held ourselves together. Somewhere, deep down, I harbor the hope that this will somehow be the beginning of our recovery from this terrible loss. That somehow, with the funeral now concluded, there will be something called "closure," as the therapists and TV commentators like to describe it. But we have just left our child lying in the rain in a grave on the side of a hill. We, her parents, are leaving her there. Soon a bulldozer will come and fill in the hole and sod will be spread across it and tamped down. In time a plaque will mark the site. Little do we realize what still lies ahead for us. There will be no closure. There will eventually be recovery, even a kind of healing, but what we do not yet realize is that despite all we have been through, the most difficult days, weeks and even years still lie ahead of us.

DREAMS AND VISITATIONS

THEY BEGAN WITHIN DAYS AFTER HER DEATH. I ENTER sleep only through exhaustion. There is no other way. Each night my mind races itself into a kind of oblivion as I inevitably play and replay the scene of her death over and over, voices dispassionate and distant echoing from the walls around me, and I eventually then fall into a state of unconsciousness. And one of two dreams or, what I have come to think of as visitations, will inevitably occur.

In the first I simply dream. There is action, like in a movie. Amateurish certainly, but there is some kind of story, or so it seems. It is in color. Allison appears happy. I am happy. Linnette is happy. We are doing things together, usually just the three of us. There is laughter and fun. She is who she always seemed to be, and we are her parents once again. She is alive. It is our ordinary world.

The second dream, however, is different. It is more like a visitation. Just the two of us. Father and daughter. In the second dream, she just sits silent and motionless before me, often in black and white, no color, her face drawn and sad, her eyes staring at me blankly, her mouth set. I am

*not actually in the dream, but somehow I seem
to be watching it happen. I am sitting looking
at her. She does not move. Now and then, however, she murmurs, "I'm sorry, I'm sorry," and I
feel myself nod and say, "It's all right. It's not your
fault. I understand."*

*Then in the dream I am suddenly sobbing and
sobbing, and soon she takes me into her arms
and holds me, like a mother holds her child, and
she says nothing more. We rock back and forth.
Back and forth. We sit and rock like this until
morning. And then I finally awaken to another
day, exhausted.*

*These dreams go on like this night after night.
I never know which one it will be. Despite the
pain and the weeping and the exhaustion, however, I have come to hope for the second dream
because then I can somehow know her as I had
not known her in life. I can touch that reservoir
of loss. I can somehow reach out into that dark
place that now holds her and quietly, so quietly,
we can somehow meet again and touch, beyond
that darkness, beyond the limited reach of our
all-too-human hands.*

CHAPTER ELEVEN

THE RITUALS IS NOW OVER AND THE GUESTS HAVE ALL GONE home, back to their own lives. We are grateful for their support and the demonstrations of affection, but we are now left largely to our own devices. It is time for Aaron to return to Seattle to the University of Washington and for Jennifer to continue her graduate studies at Portland State. They both carry burdens with them that we can never entirely know or understand.

I have not been back in the office since I walked out in tears over a week ago. Linnette is now on sick leave, having exhausted the few days of bereavement leave she was allowed. I call Bob, the attorney with whom I share office space, and he assures me he has the "barking dogs" at bay and under control. He is referring to all the open files sitting on my desk. He offers his continuing condolences and tells me how bad he felt when his aunt died. I ask him how old she was when she died, and he says she was very elderly. I know he means well, but I struggle with such analogies. Clearly, I am in no condition to return to work at this point and neither is Linnette.

The days immediately following the funeral meld together. The cold bite of March is gone and spring is making itself known. There has been some rain, light April showers for the most part, and we have been back to the cemetery several times to check on the gravesite. When we left from the funeral on Saturday the grave had not been closed. It is a shock for us to now see it just a soggy mound of dirt and sod, with the sagging flower arrangements from the service still lying across it in disarray. We stand quietly for a few moments, mindful of what and who lies beneath our feet, and then we turn and leave.

When we bought the burial plots we also chose a granite plaque as a grave marker, along with a brass urn for flowers. We chose a simple plaque, which would have only Allison's name and the dates of her birth and death. We also asked that a single rose be carved to one side. Yesterday, a week after the funeral, we visited the grave and there was the plaque and urn in place and the ground leveled, cleared and fresh sod had been laid. The carved rose is like a representation of the ones we left on her casket. Linnette comments on the small silver rose that was found near her body on the Turnpike. The one we had never seen before and could not identify. The one still folded into the manila envelope with the twisted rings, the necklace and the coins and tucked away in a drawer of mementos. We have some sense that, with these little touches, somehow we are doing the right things but are never quite sure. We just stumble along as best we can.

Today we take my parents for their first visit to the gravesite since the funeral. They are both very elderly and have difficulty navigating the uneven ground. We slowly help them down the hillside from the upper parking lot to the gravesite. It has been raining, but the sky has cleared for a few moments for which we are grateful. The grass has been newly mowed and we can see the tracks of the mower running between the grave markers. Linnette and I stand off to one side as they stare down at the plaque and read Allison's name and dates of birth and death. Two old people. We can only imagine what is going through their minds. Why her? Why not one of us? That is what they must be thinking. Linnette and I have thought the same thing many times. Why not one of us?

But then my mother begins babbling mindlessly about a childhood friend of hers, Edie, who drowned as a teen-ager in the Red River in Winnipeg, Manitoba, in the 1920s. She goes on and on. My father tries to get her back to the present and suggests perhaps he should say a prayer, but she won't stop talking. She is my mother. She suffers dementia. There is nothing I can do to stop her. Linnette and I just walk away and begin our ascent up the hill back to the car, leaving them to get back to the car as best they can. We, in effect, abandon them. Finally my father corrals my mother and they slowly follow us and we load them into the back seat and leave the stillness of the cemetery, back onto the bustle of the freeway, and slowly head east toward town. My mother continues to babble on, now in tears over the loss of her girlhood friend. Allison's death has apparently opened up a reservoir of grief locked into her memory and held in check all these years. She is no longer able to differentiate the two. It is clear we must now take care of my parents, emotionally as well as physically. And at the worst possible time.

As the weeks move on and summer approaches, Linnette and I begin visiting the gravesite almost daily, rain or shine. It becomes a sort of ritual. Sometimes we come together, sometimes alone. Sometimes we take flowers, sometimes we just arrive, and sometimes we even bring something to eat if the weather is nice and we can sit on the grass next to her and picnic. And we are often not alone. We notice others doing much the same thing. Like all newcomers, we check out the neighboring gravesites with young occupants. Ting Lee was 21 years old when he died. We don't know the cause of his death but his mother visits almost daily too. She burns incense and chants. Matt lies near Allison, not more than ten feet away. He was seventeen and also died in a car crash. By coincidence, we know his parents.

We are surprised by the number of children and young people buried here. There is something oddly comforting in that discovery. Their parents and other relatives visit regularly, like us. Some say they have been coming for years. On especially pleasant days it is rather like a gathering of the clan, an extended family of sorts. While we nod in tacit recognition but have little to say to one another, we have come to know in a special way these parents and the children and young people we had never met in life. We are a community of sorts. Strangers held together by a child's death.

THE HOMECOMING

IT IS NEAR MIDNIGHT WHEN WE ARE BOTH AWAKENED by the front door opening, the screen door slamming shut, laughter and the sound of a flight bag rolling across the living room floor, then bumping up the steps to her bedroom next to ours. In the dark of our bedroom we reach for each other. Soon the soulful sounds of "Me and Bobby McGee" drift into our bedroom as we lie breathless in the dark waiting. She is home again. Back from Paris. Back from London. Asia. Back from New York. Home again.

Moments later the light in the bathroom goes on. We can both see its glow beneath our closed door. We hear her voice talking on the phone. More laughter. She is preparing to go out. Fresh make-up after a long, late flight across the country. A party. We hear a car motor rumbling into the driveway. Mr. Right for the Summer here to take her dancing.

Then there is the clatter of high heels going down the stairs, more giggling, the front door opening and closing, the screen door slamming shut. And then as quickly as she came, she is

*gone once more. The house goes silent again. We
lie in each other arms until morning, until at last
the real world reclaims us once again.*

CHAPTER TWELVE

WE ALL, IT SEEMS, ABSORB BASIC SURVIVAL TECHNIQUES FROM early childhood. For Linnette and for me survival techniques are profoundly different. To look at us no one would think so. We have, after all these years of marriage, been described as "two peas in a pod," a description we both despise, despite our enduring love for one another.

Linnette grew up in a family that was, in significant ways, somewhat isolated and in certain ways dependent on itself. Her family environment shaped to some extent her worldview. In addition to her older sister, Barbara, she has a younger sister, Glenda, who was born with profound birth defects as a result of oxygen deprivation. As a result she is unable to speak beyond grunts and gestures, and has increasing difficulty walking or moving about as she ages. She has been in state care since she was a teenager.

When Glenda lived at home she was, of necessity, the focal point of the family. Children with severe special needs were viewed differently in those days, and it was difficult for the family to engage in many outside activities, trips or events that did not include her. As a result they were limited in their activities outside the immediate family. This is not to say they were not involved with extended family and friends, but the prime focus was serving the ongoing needs of this special child. As a result, when Allison died Linnette instinctively seemed to turn naturally inward toward family and close friends for her support. Family is and was, the primary source of her solace and strength.

I grew up in a very different family environment, despite the fact that Linnette and I appear to be alike in so many ways. We are both of white European extraction, middle or lower-middle class, come from two parent families with a stay-at-home mom and a dad who worked outside the home. But despite those similarities, the internal family dynamics were very different. My father is a minister, and we grew up with the church congregation as our family. Being immigrants from another country, we had no relations in the United States and saw relatives only rarely. The church community was, in effect, our extended family. And that community was engaged in the wider world through mission work and connections to other church congregations. My father is a proponent of what has been called the "Social Gospel," which advocates addressing the needs of the poor and the dispossessed. The family of man. Our perspective is, therefore, outward rather than inward. Instead of a family vision, I grew up with a broader world vision. One of reaching out rather than turning in.

As a result, when Allison died, my basic survival instinct was to turn outward and to attempt to lose myself in outreach and service to others beyond the family. This manifested itself in a number of ways and has evolved over time following Allison's death. That is not to say that I wish to dismiss the needs of my family or disregard them. It is just to say that I have discovered and fall back on a profound need to extend myself outward in ways and to an extent I had not before her death.

These differences in basic instincts of survival at times create conflict. It is difficult for Linnette to understand my need to reach out and difficult for me to understand her need to turn inward to family. We are each doing what we have instinctively been raised to do in an effort to save ourselves, however. We have no choice in the matter.

That we continue to survive, not just as individuals, but as a couple, is, I believe, due more to Linnette's ability to accept and tolerate my need to reach out to others than my adjustment to hers. I think, in some ways at least, her world as a teacher is more orderly than mine in the private practice of the law. I am self-employed and utterly dependent on attracting clients and maintaining my business. She, on the other hand, has the steadiness of a job, with its paycheck and the ongoing support of co-workers, as well as her commitment to and love for her young students. In any event, as the weeks go by I find myself increasingly unable to relate to my clients and their legal problems, which is at the heart of what I do. I find myself unable to relate to their needs as being more important than my own. Their legal difficulties often seem trivial to me.

This morning a young divorced man comes in to see me about the fact that his ex-wife had filed a motion with the court to amend their divorce decree to increase his child support obligation from $50 per month for each of three children in her custody, to $75 per month for each. I review his divorce decree, along with the affidavit attached to her motion for modification and make an analysis of his monthly expenses and income, as compared to when the divorce was granted. He is very angry with the ex-wife and certain she is just trying to "take me to the cleaners," as they so often put it. "She'll just spend it in the bars," he insists.

After completing my analysis I suggest to him that he should, perhaps, make a counteroffer. He nods and waits for me to suggest what an appropriate offer might be. "I would suggest you counteroffer one hundred dollars per month for each child." I can see the numbers adding up in his head. He then bursts out once the calculation had been completed, "But that's more than she's asking. What are you, nuts?" He quickly gathers up his papers and storms out of the office, slamming the door behind him. I can hear the outer door slam as well. Ann comes in to see if I am all right. I am just sitting there thinking how his problem is not a problem at all. In my view, he can afford to pay even more than she is asking and at least he has his children to support. His children deserve whatever support he can reasonably provide. I have lost my child.

As I sit there and think over what has just happened, I realize I am feeling sorry for myself. I cannot invest sufficient emotion and attention to the needs of my clients. They deserve that investment, and I am not able to provide it. It is not enough to simply know the law and to be willing to do the work. The relationship demands more of me.

In the weeks after Allison died I have found the most passion I feel for the practice of law and for my clients in pro bono work. I have become involved with the Volunteer Lawyer Project in Multnomah County, a project of the local bar association. It pairs pro bono private lawyers with low-income clients in civil matters, such as landlord-tenant, debt collections, car sales and the like; matters where the individual is not entitled to court-appointed counsel, but cannot afford to hire a lawyer. In other words, I am, in those instances, the lawyer of last resort for a desperate client. If I don't represent that client, it is unlikely anyone else will. It is only in that situation where the need is so desperate that I find I can again generate the enthusiasm, focus and energy necessary to overcome my own grief and sense of loss to legally represent others. As a result, I find myself taking on more and more of these cases, to the detriment of my private for-fee practice. As rewarding as these cases are, I need to earn money and cannot afford to donate all of my time. Thus I feel increasingly caught in a trap. A trap of my own making. Finally it occurs to me that a change is somehow going to have to be made or I fear I will literally go insane. It has become that serious. My basic instincts of reaching out are finally being met by representing the most needy. It is what I believe I must continue to do to survive. But I can't afford to do that which may be essential to my own recovery.

CHAPTER THIRTEEN

WHILE I HAD NOT IN THE YEARS JUST PRIOR TO ALLISON'S
death been sedentary in any sense, playing tennis, for
example, several times a week, about six months before
her death I suddenly, for no apparent reason, felt I needed
to do a daily walk. No matter the weather, snow, wind,
rain or sunshine, I would leave the house early before the
start of my workday and walk to Glendoveer Golf Course,
where there is a two-mile bark-dust covered path encircling
the golf course. The path winds around through wooded
areas and along straight-aways. The walk from our house
in Parkrose to the starting point is a mile each way. Consequently, my morning walk is about four miles, done in fifty
minutes to an hour, depending on the weather conditions.

Why I suddenly decided I needed to do this I do not
know. It was as if a toggle switch had been thrown in my
head. One minute, I was sitting on the couch watching reruns
or sports on television, the next minute I had an undeniable
and compulsive need to walk. And not just to walk daily, but

to walk with purpose. By the time we received the dreadful news of Allison's death, I was in the best physical shape I had been in years, my weight down to exactly what was appropriate for my height and body mass index.

While I cannot say I had some sort of premonition of Allison's death, or even of some other awful event requiring me to have such a reserve of energy and stamina, because I did not, I nonetheless cannot help but feel I was being prepared in some way for such a happening. I am not sure I would have or could have survived the shock of her dying if I had not.

And so even now I continue to walk as I try to reconcile her death to our new life without her. Each morning, rain or shine, I leave the house and trudge to the path, walk around it, greeting the regulars as they greet me. I know none of them by name, although we might, on occasion, stop to chat if the weather is unusually pleasant. There are young and old, slim and not so slim. There are a number of attractive women, many in tight spandex jogging gear. Often as one passes by me I find myself unconsciously speeding up my pace. I justify this by thinking that it increases my heart rate. The only folks who are not so glad to see us are the golfers, who cruise around from hole to hole in their electric golf carts and pretend they too are getting some exercise. They puff on big cigars and look over at us walkers and joggers with disdain.

Over time I have learned that path intimately. I have come to personally know the rabbits that live in the woods surrounding the golf course, rabbits that had no doubt been let loose by someone who could not or would not care for them any longer. Beneath the "Please don't feed the rabbits" sign posted by the Multnomah County

Parks Department, we leave little offerings of lettuce or carrots. I have learned where the mushrooms grow in their proper season. I see the vine maples turn in the fall. I discover trilliums growing in late winter or early spring. Once there was a used condom draped across the bark dust looking lost and forlorn and utterly depleted. I can only imagine the discomfort that particular set of participants must have endured for whatever brief moment of pleasure it might have provided.

The path changes with the seasons. In summer it is hot, and we all walk around sucking on bottles of water and sweating. The old men wear sweatbands around their balding heads and pretend they are real jocks. The real jocks don't bother. The bunnies are listless and lie to one side, out of the traffic pattern, begging as usual, but without enthusiasm, their back legs stretched straight out behind them. In fall the deciduous trees lose their leaves, and the landscape opens up and one can see through the bare trees the uniformity of housing developments across 147th Street. In winter, especially with snow on the ground, the woods lose their color and are black and white, or sepia, like an old yellowed photograph, beautiful but somehow ominous. And by another spring, the woods are again becoming lush and green. There might even be flowerbeds of daffodils growing in patches, the handiwork of someone who can't leave a piece of bare ground unadorned.

It may be too much to say that walking the path has saved me, but in a sense it has. Both by giving me the exercise I need to stay at full physical strength to endure what needs to be endured, and an opportunity to find myself daily in this microcosm of my own new world. A world that is both changing and constant. From season to season, and from day to day. A time for walking by myself, a time to be alone, a time to reconnect to my body, to meditate. It has become for me, over time, my path to the future.

THE BEDROOM

"Flesh is merely a lesson.
We learn it & pass on."
Erica Jong

AT NIGHT WE LIE IN THE DARK OF OUR BEDROOM, LIS-tening. At night her bedroom, next to ours, still throbs with her presence. Sounds emanate out of the silence as if she were still alive. We do not understand how it can be.

Incredulous, we hold hands beneath the bed-clothes, struggling for some kind of peace, trying at times just to catch our breath from all that has occurred. The days are hell.... But the nights worse.

At night her bedroom is there, waiting, alive as ever, next to our own. But during the day it just simply exists as the container of all her things: the posters hung on the wall of rock groups she adored; the floppy hat she wore to her high school senior prom hanging from a nail on the wall; music tapes thrown in a jumble into a box next to the tape-deck we bought for her last birthday; and lying on the dresser those white, formal gloves from the senior prom that still hold the shape of her hands. Her clothes lie in heaps on the floor where she dropped them. Shoes creased and cracked where over time her feet had broken the leather. The bed remains unmade, the tangled sheets somehow waiting for her return. We cannot seem to perform even this simple task. It is too final.

During the day, however, we often slip into her room just to sit for a while, sometimes alone, sometimes together. The difference in daytime is the stillness of the air. The quietness. No radio blaring. No laughter. No sounds of her rushing to the bathroom to check out a new hairstyle or try on a new blush. No endless flurry of her changing clothes, getting ready to go out.

For a while we had hoped, in some deep place of retreat, that she would return. We waited patiently, even expectantly. And in a sense, allowing ourselves that touch of insanity kept us sane. Within the madness of her death, we needed to embrace some small moment of disbelief, some quiet place, not unlike her daytime bedroom, where we could go to flee the reality of what and who had been taken from us so suddenly and with such violence.

But at night the room comes alive again. I lie in our bed, the headboard next to our common wall with her room, and I can feel the vibrations of her moving about. I can hear sounds *emanating from the darkness of her coming and going, doors slamming, stiletto heels clattering in the hallway and down the stairs. The thumping sound of a flight bag being dragged up the steps. Even loud music from the stereo. It's party time.*

But despite all I know, it is not so. The room only lives like this so long as we remain locked in our need for her. And as we perceive, her need for us.

The room, we know is a memorial. There have been those who have suggested we should have cleared it out immediately after her death. "Get rid of what is just a painful reminder of her," they say in all compassion and concern for us.

They do not understand. It is like living with an arrow in your heart. It is the knowing infliction of a pain we can endure in order to relieve a pain that is unendurable.

And so it remains as it was. Her clothes still hang in the closet. Her airline uniforms, pressed and ready for use. However, as the days and nights pass she is gradually now entering into a more perfect state. In time it seems that what we have lost is becoming part of who we are. We mourn our separateness from her but, in the process, we are becoming her. She is becoming us. We are gradually, night by night, visitation by visitation, becoming the world she would have been.

CHAPTER FOURTEEN

"What falls away is always.
And is near."

Deborah Tall, *A Family of Strangers*

THIS IS, IN A SENSE, OUR FIRST DEATH. A DEATH WE DEEPLY
and persistently grieve. Our parents are all living, although
in various stages of decline. My father, Mark, has had
heart problems for years, starting with a heart attack in
his fifties, and now diabetes. He is now eighty-nine. My
mother, Nan, had a serious stroke in her early fifties and
subsequently, less serious strokes, and it has significantly
affected her short-term memory and personality. She is
almost eighty. Linnette's mother, Nancy, is in good health
and fully active. She is seventy-six. Linnette's father, Al,
is already deeply lost to Alzheimer's dementia, although
he still lives at home with Nancy, and it appears he understands nothing of what has taken place. Our siblings are
all living, again in various states of health. My brother,

Doug, has MS, and is somewhat restricted. Linnette's younger sister, Glenda, has been profoundly disabled since birth and lives in an adult group home.

As a result, this death, Allison's death, is our first of anyone close whose death would be unanticipated. My grandfathers and my paternal grandmother were gone before I was born. My maternal grandmother, known as Gram, died at age 90. Linnette's grandparents also died in old age. The Chinese have a blessing that I had never before understood. But I do now. They say:

> *Grandparents die,*
> *Parents, die,*
> *Children die.*

How, I wondered, can the deaths in families be considered a blessing, as a general proposition? But now I know that, since we all die eventually, when family members die in generational order that is a blessing. When they die out of order, that is a curse. Allison's death is a curse. The order has been broken.

And so we struggle, trying to come to grips with her absence. Linnette is off from school for the summer, which may or may not be good for her. I think it is good, as it gives her time for herself, without the strain and stress of having to pull herself together each weekday morning and trudge off to face a class of 3rd graders all anxious for her attention and energy. Energy she no longer has. I have been urging her to consider taking an indefinite leave of absence in the fall until she feels ready to go back into the classroom. I have my doubts that she will do that, however. And I suspect her work with the children outweighs her considerations for herself. They are her family too, no matter whether they speak English, or not. Whether they are special needs kids, or not. This past year she has had five different languages being spoken in her classroom, as well as several autistic children. Next year won't be any easier. She will, of course, have no assistant to help her.

We have all had some family counseling at Kaiser Permanente, and Linnette has had some sessions with a psychiatrist who has prescribed some antidepressants for her, which seem to be helping tremendously. But pills don't take the place of lost children.

I think Linnette is more attuned to her state and degree of disability than I am. She seems more willing to seek out help. Perhaps I am in denial. To some extent that is no doubt true. Being self-employed and being a lawyer, one to whom others turn for help dealing with certain kinds of problems, I am schooled, in a sense, not to show weakness or uncertainty. As a result it is difficult, at times, for me to admit my needs emotionally. No client wants a lawyer ready to dissolve at a moment's notice when the going gets tough. And so I strive to hold it together, not realizing how impaired I really am. It will become more apparent to me as I return more fully to my law practice.

In addition to all that is the need to continue to earn money so that bills can get paid. I have responsibilities for overhead at the office. A secretary who needs to be paid for her work, rent, maintaining our law library, professional fees and other expenses. They go on no matter what. I am not in a financial position to stop working, to stop maintaining my practice that I have spent close to twenty years building.

Just the other day my father, sensing our financial

situation, invited me over and sat down with me and offered to give me $5,000. We have just paid for all of Allison's expenses, Mr. Mack in New Jersey, the funeral home here, the cemetery, the burial costs, and I have not been in the office now for several weeks, other than one time, when I went in, sat at my desk for about twenty minutes staring at the piles of files on my desk, burst into tears and left. So I accept his offer with gratitude especially for his taking the initiative, and for his thoughtfulness and generosity.

And in a way, this is the first truly significant death for him, my mother and my in-laws as well. The first death of a grandchild, or at least one who had lived. My sister gave birth to a baby boy, Derek, who died at birth. In looking back I now realize how little support we gave her and my brother-in-law, Paul, when that happened. The birth occurred just weeks before Linnette and I were married in 1960. We were all so caught up in the wedding plans that summer that the death of little Derek was not acknowledged to the extent it should have been. Knowing how removed we were emotionally from her loss makes me more forgiving of those around us now who are, for one reason or another, not able to give us the support or the attention we would like.

Grandparents die,
Parents die,
Children die.

CHAPTER FIFTEEN

IT IS EARLY MAY. WE ARE VISITING WITH LINNETTE'S PARENTS, Al and Nancy, on the farm. The farm is twenty acres where Al grew Christmas trees until Alzheimer's disease robbed him of much of his rational mind. Al retired from the Portland Fire Department as soon as he was eligible. Fighting fires was what he did to earn a paycheck. But his heart lay elsewhere. He was, at heart, a farmer. Perhaps this need reaches back into his Tennessee country roots. He and Nancy bought the land adjacent to acreage owned and occupied by Barbara and Thor, Linnette's sister and brother in law, and built a lovely home. They then sold the house where Linnette had lived since her birth until she and I married, and moved. The acreage is in the tiny community of Helvetia, what some call the Little Switzerland of Oregon, an area of open rolling hills. There Al worked the land, never making much money, but never needing much. He spent his days nursing the rows of trees into sufficient growth to be ready for market each

Christmas season. He was such a poor business he probably lost money each year. But he loved it.

But then the memory began to fade and the disease became more and more noticeable, at least to the rest of the family. Not to Nancy, however, who continued to care for him and to deny his affliction for as long as she could. He is deep into dementia now, and she in denial when we sit at their dining room table this afternoon, drinking coffee and looking out at the now overgrown yard, the yard he can no longer maintain, Christmas trees in the distance now neglected and growing wild. We are, of course, talking about Allison and how we miss her and what her future might have been had she lived, the potential grandchildren we will now not have, nor the pleasure of growing old with her as our daughter. Al is sitting off to one side, not part of the conversation, just staring blankly out the window. Suddenly he turns to me and says, "Well, now you won't have to pay for a wedding."

It is like he has slammed his fist into my heart. No one, however inept in their desire to comfort us, has ever said anything so cruel. So totally insensitive. My initial instinct is to want to strike him back. But he is my own father-in-law. An old and sick man. I cannot believe that anyone could be so demented, so unconnected to reality that they would say something like that. I literally have to restrain myself. Never in my adult life have I come so close to physical violence.

Instead I get up from the table and walk down the hall, past the bedrooms and into the bathroom. I have to get away from him. At this moment, I cannot even look at him. I stand in the bathroom, staring into the vanity mirror, trying to calm myself. Gradually I convince myself, he is old, he is demented, he has no idea what he is saying, he no longer even knows who Allison is or was. He may not even know who we are. We may just be strangers sitting at his table. Little by little I compose myself and return to the dining room. He is now sitting in his old recliner chair in the living room, just staring up at the vaulted ceiling. I tell Linnette it is time to leave.

Shortly after that encounter the decision is finally made by Nancy, with the help of the family, to place Al in a nursing home facility. He has begun wandering more and more, and several times has become lost and has been brought home by the police, or Nancy has received calls from business owners saying he is with them and doesn't seem to know where he is. One time he was in a café in the Linton District on the outskirts of the industrial area of Portland, far from Helvetia, not far from where he had once lived as a boy. He was apparently trying to find his way home to his mother. Unfortunately, the home he was trying to find no longer existed except in his diminished mind. To be so disconnected from the world and yet to have to live in it must surely be a kind of hell. To not even know you have lost a granddaughter is its own tragedy.

CHAPTER SIXTEEN

"In grief there is no hiding."

Stephen Levine, *Who Dies?*

Over time it seems the process of grieving is a process of giving birth to oneself. Tears and pain gradually diminish. The unexpected sobs occur less frequently. Little by little, over the months that follow, I find occasional moments of pleasure. Even joy at times. At first I felt great guilt over such moments. How could I feel pleasure when my daughter had been taken from me? I could see that grave lying open in the rain. Sodden flowers strewn about. Was this a betrayal? How could I? And if Linnette seems to have a momentary smile, other than, perhaps, a recollection of something from Allison's past, how could she? I feel resentment. Sometimes flashes of anger. I think perhaps she does too, seeing me take pleasure in something.

Linnette and I have played tennis for many years. We belong to the Irvington Tennis Club and play often.

Yesterday evening I went to the club to join the guys in a couple of sets of doubles. Our customary Tuesday evening game. I was standing on the court, in position at the net, my partner ready to serve, when I suddenly burst into tears. What in God's name was I doing here? How can I justify having fun. I just buried my daughter. I played through to the end of the session, tears streaming down my face, but could barely see the ball coming at me. I am angry with myself. I have no right to be doing something as frivolous as playing a game under these circumstances. I leave the club thinking I may never step onto a tennis court again.

I have also come to realize how much in my life is now fantasy. The fantasy that Allison will, in some way, at some time, actually be coming home. The fantasy I have that the young blonde girl walking down the street ahead of me will suddenly turn around and greet me and it will be Allison. Or that girl at the head of the line at a McDonald's waiting to order a hamburger. Or on the MAX train, that young woman I see getting off at Pioneer Square whose walk seems so familiar, and I have a sudden impulse to run after her just to make sure it isn't Allison and that we have somehow missed each other.

And the bizarre ways Linnette and I discuss our lives and our parental responsibilities with Allison now gone. Shortly after her death we had a conversation that on the surface appeared to us as rational as discussing a grocery list of what we needed to buy at the Safeway store for dinner. One of us, and I don't recall which, said, in all seriousness, that one of us should commit suicide in order to be with Allison. That she might need one of us. Later Linnette will tell me she doesn't recall this conversation, but I do because of the strange gulf that clearly existed between reason and fantasy but which also somehow merged in our minds at that time as a sensible thing for parents to be contemplating. I recall how calm we were in discussing the necessity of our own deaths. No hysteria. No wringing of hands.

We talked it over, as parents are supposed to do in considering the needs of their children, and finally decided that to do so would be too harmful to our surviving children and to the grandchildren we hoped to have someday. We knew they needed us. We did not know if Allison needed us or not. *"It's okay. I'm all right."* In the end, we discarded the idea and never discussed it again. It is only looking back I realize how insane it was to even think about it.

NIGHT WORK

WHEN WE ARE AT HOME DURING THE WORKWEEK much of our overt grieving happens at night. We have come to call it our "night work". And work it is. Linnette lies on her side of the bed and I lie on mine. The headboard of our bed leans up against the wall adjoining Allison's bedroom. It is as if we are somehow touching her in the dark. We both know we have to be at our jobs in the morning and we struggle to sleep. At times we are desperate to sleep. But even when we finally fall asleep it seems we are still working through her death and the terrible loss of a life not fully lived.

We beg to fall asleep, knowing we have work commitments in the morning. A class full of eager children for Linnette. Trials and hearings for me. Clients and judges and opposing counsel. Linnette tosses in the dark on one side and I on the other. Sometimes we hold each other, sometimes we want to be as far away from each other as the bed will allow. I can sometimes feel Allison's presence through the wallboard. Sometimes I think I can hear her, laughing, talking, moving about. Then I finally fall into sleep. And that seems the best description of it. I "fall" into sleep. We do not

*drift off quietly. Rather it seems we just descend
into unconsciousness. A kind of troubled coma.*

*There seems to be no solution for our trou-
bled nights. Linnette has some medication which
she says helps. I have resisted that route so far.
There is something inside me that actually invites
this nightly grief process, despite my feelings of
despair and helplessness. Somehow I need this
sense of connection with her. During the day
there is no sense of life in the house or in her bedroom. It is just dead air. But at night it is different
and I reenter her life, Part of me needs that connection. Perhaps that is another lesson of grief,
that we keep our dead child alive in various ways
for as long as we can, however painful.*

CHAPTER SEVENTEEN

IT IS ONE MONTH TO THE DAY SINCE ALLISON WAS KILLED. IT IS a Sunday. It is the second Sunday in May. It is Mother's Day. There is no alternative but to face it head on. It is Linnette's first Mother's Day without her. Over the past few years Allison might have been in Paris, or Calcutta, or Barcelona, if not New York or here. Today she is nowhere. But in our thoughts. Jennifer and Aaron do their best to bridge the loss, and they are the solace Linnette needs at this time. But there is still always the missing one. The one who will always be missing.

We go to the cemetery late in the morning with flowers, small, pink roses, like the roses we left on her coffin when it was closed three weeks ago. The ground has settled around the grave and the sod is beginning to look like it belongs there. The plaque and the brass urn are now in place. I trudge up the hill to the flower room for water and we place the flowers in the urn and stand back, holding each other, just looking down at the lettering in the granite, the name, the dates of birth and death. The cemetery is filled with visitors, many with flowers, many dressed as if they had just come from church or synagogue. Jessica's family is standing over her grave. There is a huge balloon always floating above it. Ting Lee's mother, is burning incense on her son's grave, just west of Allison's. She is weeping and moaning. She is alone.

Later we have a quiet family dinner. We have done what we can. There is no alternative but to face what comes. I think to myself, Father's Day is not far off. How will I deal with it? How will I deal with the failure that I feel from not having been able to protect Allison from what happened. It is a thought that haunts me. That's what fathers are supposed to do. They protect their children. Reason tells me what happened had nothing to do with my ability or inability to protect her. But deep inside, my DNA tells me, I failed her. I will have to deal with that failure forever. Perhaps Linnette, in some sense, feels the same way. It is not anything we have discussed. But I see the pain of this occasion on her face, in her eyes, in the language of her body.

Soon, at least, school will be over and she will not have to get up every morning and prepare herself for another day in the classroom. After a quiet dinner with family, our parents leave, my folks back to their little house just blocks away, and Linnette's parents to their home in Helvetia, many miles away. Tomorrow will be another day of work. I think I have a trial starting, but I'm not sure. Normally I would be nervous as a cat, pacing the house rehearsing my opening statement and worrying that my witnesses will all show up. Tonight I'm not even certain which courthouse it is in.

We get ready for bed and another night of listening to the empty room next to our own.

CHAPTER EIGHTEEN

THE FIRST HALF OF THE MONTH OF JUNE HAS ALWAYS BEEN family oriented. June 11th is Linnette's birthday and June 12th is Jennifer's. These days are followed closely by Father's Day. Each of these occasions is yet another opportunity to experience our loss. On the weekend of the birthdays we make our pilgrimage to the cemetery. The weather has turned, and the days begin to warm. The Rose Festival, Portland's huge annual celebration, is underway. This is the weekend of the famous Rose Parade. The city is all flowers, floats and marching bands. We fight the crowds to get across town to the cemetery. From the bridge over the Willamette River, viewing the downtown area and the waterfront festivities, it looks like everyone in the world is having a good time.

The cemetery is a vast green lawn. The headstones are flat with the ground, so it is easy to mow, and we can see the tracks left by the mowers. For some reason I find it disturbing that they run directly across Allison's grave. It seems an intrusion, a sort of violation of her space. We place flowers in the urn and stand in silence. We are alone here today. There is a new grave about ten yards away, disheveled stands of flowers strewn around it, and I discover it is the grave of a man I used to know when I worked for Multnomah County. I pay my respects. Then we leave.

The birthday celebrations are muted affairs this year. We do our best to keep our spirits up for the sake of the birthday girls, but it isn't easy. But somehow we get through it.

This is followed by Father's Day. I have been dreading it. But, like everything else, it comes anyway. Aaron is off from school and home for the summer. So we have family together. We will have my parents and Linnette's parents over to the house for dessert in the late afternoon. There will be the usual exchange of gifts for the fathers. Linnette and I have made our trip to the cemetery earlier in the day and again stood quietly for a few moments of silence.

For me these are moments of irrational guilt. I castigate myself for my failures as a father. While others may think this is a time of celebration of fatherhood in general, for me it is the opposite. Some part of me proclaims: You have failed. And now it is too late. Here you stand at your daughter's grave. What greater failure could there be than that?

CHAPTER NINETEEN

IT IS NOW LATE JUNE. SCHOOL IS FINALLY OUT AND LINNETTE no longer needs to drag herself off to work each morning. I have been back to work but go about my tasks listlessly. And now the house seems to close in on us. We make the decision to take the Volkswagen camper and get out of town. We decide to head east, up the Columbia River Gorge, to where, we don't know, and for no particular reason. Since I was partially raised in Eastern Oregon, I may subconsciously be trying to take myself to a time and place when and where my life was more orderly and safe. Somehow it is comforting to feel we can get away from the house, and the city, and to just be on the open road with no destination in mind To be transient.

We set off on a bright, sunny morning and head east up the Gorge, along the river, past Crown Point, through Hood River, and The Dalles. We reach the Biggs Junction and, on a whim, cross over the Columbia into the State of Washington and head north, through the Tri-Cities area, toward Ritzville and Spokane. This is not a route we have ever taken before. The countryside broadens out into vast rolling hills of wooded countryside, ranches and wheat fields, and the weather turns hot and dry.

We spend our first night in a motel outside of Ritzville, an adequate but unremarkable lodging. The next morning we eat breakfast at a local Denny's and get on the road again. The second night we plan to stay in Spokane, and after driving around and familiarizing ourselves with the city, we find a spot near the river to camp for the night. It is not an official campground, but rather a large, paved parking lot. There are no signs saying we can't spend the night, so we pull the drapes on the van, pull down the bed and sack out.

The next morning we watch the sun rising up out of the river, reflecting a stream of silver threading through the city. We lie in the camper, with the drapes pulled back and just follow the sun's assent up into the clear blue of the Eastern Washington sky. We have not talked about Allison in the past two days but we each know that internal conversations are going on. Outwardly we are calm. But I know I survive each day with a stab to the heart. Each new day feels like a knife wound that will not close or heal. We are now students of grief.

At home we continue to go to the cemetery and leave flowers. As the weather has improved we lengthen our stay and linger longer. We sit by her grave and just chat with each other, and with her. The broad expanse of green lawn that stretches out from her gravesite remains clipped and edged. Squirrels and blue jays cavort in the big blue spruce that offers her shade from the heat. It continues to be a place of life and death. It is becoming a home away from home.

But for now, here in the unfamiliar landscape of Eastern Washington, I feel somehow briefly divorced from that reality. Disconnected. Now we are just here with one another, waking to the sunrise, preparing to go to breakfast and take to the road again, this time on to Idaho, Coeur d' Lane at the northern tip of the lake.

It is a short drive to Coeur d' Alene, Idaho. Coeur d' Alene Lake is vast and lovely. Again we find a spot to park the camper and plan on spending the night. That evening we walk along the lake shore and watch the pleasure boats coming and going, their running lights sparkling in the night air like diamonds. There seems to be some sort of gathering of restored Chris-Craft boats, with the boat people shouting back and forth to one another as their boats pass by. Were it not for the pressing sense of loss that hangs over us the setting would be romantic. We see other couples, many of them young, hand in hand, strolling past. Honeymooners. I wonder what realities they might be living with beneath the calmness of the evening. Or what realities they will, in time, have to live with. Can they see the dark, heavy cloud that seems to float above us?

Little by little the dark circles etched beneath Linnette's eyes are beginning to fade away. Whether it is the travel or just that she no longer needs to go off to work each day, I don't know. We hold one another as we huddle through the night in the double sleeping bag. Even here, in the camper, we are surrounded by memories of past family camping trips. Aaron sleeping in the pup tent, the girls in the larger tent and Mom and Dad in the queen-sized bed, snug in the camper. We laugh when we remember how the girls, on our first camping trip years ago, looked in vain for an electrical outlet in their tent in order to plug in a hair dryer. We talk of the storm that struck as we were camped at Fort Worden, near Port Townsend, Washington, that last summer before Jennifer married and left home for good. The flashes of lightning, the rain and wind that buffeted the tents and rocked the van. Such memories flood back to haunt us and, in an odd way, comfort us. Somehow, here alone in a strange place, we feel, nonetheless, a sense of family. Both living children and the one no longer living now occupy only our memories here. In this strange way, we are all together again.

CHAPTER TWENTY

I HAVE BROUGHT WITH ME SEVERAL BOOKS OF RICHARD HUGO'S poetry, which include his many poems written from and about the towns of the Pacific Northwest, Montana (where he taught), Idaho, and Washington (where he was born and raised). Hugo could drive through a small town and write about it as if he had lived there for years. Although I have never been in these places before, I am seeing all the familiar names, like Missoula, Butte, Deer Lodge and Wisdom. Wallace and Kellogg. Billings and Bozeman. They live for me in Dick's poems.

While we did not purposely set out to drive through these towns, following any particular route, we find ourselves passing though them nonetheless. Each evening I read a poem or two about the next town we might come across as I peruse the map. In each town there is inevitably a bar, several churches in semi-ruin, a shabby school and a few meager houses or cabins here and there, surrounded by vast areas of rangeland with cattle roaming free. Dick tended to spend a good deal of his time in those bars, where he met the locals and could soak up the local lore along with the beer.

I remember being with him at Lake Wilderness in Western Washington years ago, when several of us closed up the Lake Wilderness tavern. We all climbed into Dick's big green Buick convertible and he insisted on driving us to Kapowsin, a town not too far away, that was the source material for his second book of poems, The Death of the Kapowsin Tavern. There we were at 2:30 a.m., cruising down the deserted main street while Dick, acting as tour director, pointed out the sights, including the charred remains of the burned-out tavern that had inspired the title poem. Given that Dick, our tour guide and driver, undoubtedly had had too much to drink suggests that the trip was ill-advised. The next morning, after I sobered up, I realized that we were all fortunate to get home alive.

So now Linnette and I are making our own travels through the desperate, endless stretch of landscape that is Eastern Idaho and on into Western Montana. We pass through Kellogg and then Wallace, a town known mostly for its past of legalized prostitution and silver mining. We join the other tourists and go down into an old silver mine. We cross over Lookout Pass, into Montana, through St. Regis and descend finally down into Missoula where we plan to spend the night and perhaps a day or two more. We still have no itinerary. It is a lovely, quiet university town, the Clark River running through it. We lunch in a local spot, one I'm sure Dick had mentioned to me at one time or another. It is easy to see why he would have felt so immediately at home here. Later I browse a bookstore and look for Dick's books, with no success. They seem oddly unaware of who he was or what he accomplished. Hugo had died suddenly in 1982 in Seattle and his local notoriety was no longer apparent by the time we got there. As is so often the case, he was better known and revered elsewhere than here in what had become his own hometown. A prophet is not without honor, save in his own home, or so the Bible says.

We take a motel room for the night in Missoula to give ourselves a chance to clean up and get a more relaxed night's sleep. The camper is fine and the bed comfortable, but we are always worried about getting rousted out by the authorities for parking illegally, and we do not have amenities, like a hot shower.

From Missoula we head south-southeast, taking less traveled back roads. We are now intent on finding Philipsburg, the setting for Dick's most famous and celebrated poem. And we do. Situated in the heart of Granite County. The knobby, rocky landscape lives up to its name. We drive into Philipsburg and it seems still very much as Dick found it and described it years earlier. Not a ghost town but close. The noose still hangs in the upper window of the jailhouse. The streets "laid out by the insane," is what he said. We drive on up the hill to the site of the mines, and they appear to be in ruins too, the buildings sunken in on themselves and collapsing to the ground.

Now we wander aimlessly. Leaving Philipsburg, we continue south, eventually finding ourselves in Big Hole just as the sun is setting. Big Hole, we learn, is the site of the sneak attack by the U.S. army on the fleeing Nez Perce Indians as the men, women and children slept by the river in their tepees. It is now an historic site.

Other than curious deer and birds of all kinds, we

are alone, the only living, human creatures. We walk the remnants of the battlefield and see the tepee poles still standing sadly, set against the dying sun as it settles behind the mountains to the west. I can almost hear the voices of the past, the drumbeat of history, the desperate sounds of battle. No one else is here to interrupt our reverie. The history plaques on the wall of the small museum on the site inform us that the Nez Perce won this battle, only to lose in another north at Bear Paw, just short of the Canadian border, which, if they had been able to cross, would have brought them to safety. I shuffle along the dusty paths, wandering among the tepees, hoping to find an arrowhead or some other relic of what had taken place here.

That night we camp near Big Hole, just pulling off the narrow highway where we find a secluded spot beneath a stand of trees near a stream. We have a dinner of food left over from earlier meals, fruit and soda pop, chips and packaged cookies.

There is something haunting about Big Hole that stays with me. We are both quiet and introspective as we pull down the bed and climb into our big sleeping bag. I get my best night's sleep of the trip so far. Maybe the best in weeks. The ghosts of Big Hole speak to me through my dreams. Our own loss seems to momentarily merge into the larger losses of the world. For the first time in weeks I feel myself once again not a mere observer of life, but a part of it. A small step has been taken.

CHAPTER TWENTY-ONE

We spend several weeks slowly making our way across the width of Montana, before arriving at the Little Big Horn, site of the Custer battle. We spend several days wandering the battle site, going through the museum, and immersing ourselves in the history of the place. The landscape is open and wide, the Little Big Horn River slowly making its way across the green meadows once the scene of hand-to-hand combat to the death. While it does not have the impact that Big Hole did, it is impressive nonetheless. Perhaps it is the crowds and the almost carnival atmosphere that makes it different. Everywhere we go there is someone taking photos and talking loudly. People on vacation, not, like us, on a pilgrimage. Big Hole was ours alone. Intimate. The Custer site is not.

From Little Big Horn we make our way down through the Crow reservation into Wyoming and eventually reach Cody, the town named for Buffalo Bill. We are surprised to find signs throughout the town in both English and

Japanese. But then we see the tour buses coming into town in droves, filled to overflowing with Japanese tourists, each seemingly with a camera and taking photos of everything Western.

This is the quintessential Western Town. Almost like a movie set for John Wayne or Gary Cooper. The next day we go to the Buffalo Bill Museum and the Remington Museum and that evening to the rodeo, a re-enactment of the Wild West Shows made famous by Buffalo Bill. The stands are filled with Japanese tourists watching the bull riding and calf roping and bucking broncos. They look at one another as if not quite knowing how to interpret what is going on. Cameras are clicking constantly. We watch a Japanese tourist wearing his new ten-gallon hat, swaying unsteadily from side to side as he walks down the main street of town wearing his shiny, new cowboy boots and his stiff new Levi's.

The next morning we head west for the first time since the trip began. Our destination is Yellowstone National Park. There have been terrible forest fires in the park and most of the entrances have been closed. Still miles away, the air is already heavy with dense smoke that can be seen hovering on the horizon long before we actually find ourselves in the park. Though many of the areas of the park are closed due to the fires, we spend several days roaming the grounds, seeing Old Faithful, and some of the other well-known sights, and finally emerge going north, back into Montana, one of the few exit/entrances still open.

Then we head west again, through southern Montana, on into southern Idaho, across to Boise, and finally cross the Oregon-Idaho border into Ontario and Malheur County. We are ready to get back home. Back to our house and our lives. Back to Jennifer and Aaron. Back to Allison. The reprieve from reality will soon be over.

From Ontario we head to Baker City and then on to La Grande, my old hometown. We spend the night in a motel on Adams Ave. and eat at a Mexican restaurant. It is clear the town is changing in its demographics since I lived here forty years ago. I recall one Chinese restaurant when I lived there as being the only foreign food restaurant in town. The next morning we drive by my old house and through the neighborhood, and take some photos of the church where my father was the pastor.

From La Grande we drive on to Pendleton, down the twists and turns of Cabbage Hill and through the Umatilla Indian Reservation. Finally we encounter, once again, the Columbia River. We know we are almost home. We retrace our path west along the river, back through The Dalles, Hood River and on into Portland. We are home again after weeks of wandering freely. I feel somewhat restored and almost ready to face what remains of the summer.

As I enter the house, however, I immediately sense the stillness. Everything is where it is supposed to be. Aaron is there to welcome us home and we call Jennifer to let her know we are back. While we escaped for a time, it was temporary at best. Linnette is off for the summer but my office, with its barking dogs, is still waiting. The plot of ground at Sunset Memorial Gardens is still there. That night we hear again the sounds we have not heard for weeks. Allison's bedroom comes alive again. Once again we lie in the dark just listening.

SIGHTINGS

It is early on a Tuesday morning, the middle of July. I am heading west on Hwy. 26 toward Hillsboro where I have a court appearance scheduled. Traffic is heavy coming into Portland but light heading out of the city. I cruise through the Vista Ridge Tunnel where just a few weeks ago Linnette and I saw graffiti painted on the rounded, gray, concrete wall, "Allison, we love you." We have never learned who did that. It is gone now, painted over.

A short distance farther west I pass beneath the green hillsides that bank up away from the freeway. Sunset Memorial Gardens. My daughter lies up there. I look up as I speed past, thinking, somehow, I might actually see her. Several days ago I was up there alone, just visiting, sitting on the grass by her side eating my lunch, and I suddenly looked up and there she was, standing off to one side, beneath that big blue spruce tree that is just a few yards from her grave. She was dressed all in white and just stood there leaning against the tree and staring at me. Her face was sad. She said nothing. When I looked up again she was gone.

It seems odd my being here now on this

freeway heading to work along with the rest of the world, knowing my daughter is just a short distance away, yet, somehow, part of another world, silent and remote. I speak her name as I pass by, and I wave.

CHAPTER TWENTY-TWO

ONE OF THE STEPS WE MUST NOW TAKE IS TO BEGIN DEALING with the legal matters surrounding Allison's death. We will need to find legal counsel. Since I am a lawyer I assume this will not be difficult. I am wrong. It proves to be very difficult. Since Allison maintained her home with us in Portland, continued to file tax returns and pay Oregon income tax, but also maintained an apartment with other flight attendants in New York, there is the question which state, if either, has jurisdiction over any action on behalf of her estate. In addition, she met her death in New Jersey. Consequently, there are three states with potential jurisdiction involved. I am too distraught to even begin to try and analyze a resolution to the conflicts of law that the facts present. We need a lawyer. Someone who can view the facts and the law issues objectively.

We are aware too that time is passing and any investigation necessary to preserve evidence from the accident scene and from the vehicle needs to be done soon or it may be lost. One of Allison's roommates in Long Beach is engaged to a New York City police detective. He recommends a trial lawyer in New York to us, one who is also licensed in New Jersey. That sounds perfect. I contact the lawyer by telephone and we have a long conversation. He claims to be very interested in representing us, even enthusiastic, and asks that I send him the police reports and other information, such as insurance coverage, and he will have his investigator get on the case right away. He agrees that evidence needs to be preserved and quickly.

The next day I send him all the material that he requested, along with my own lengthy statement of the facts from our end of the continent. That is the last we will hear from him. Several weeks pass and there is no response. Knowing from personal experience the tendency of some attorneys to procrastinate, I begin to telephone his office. He is never available to talk. It is apparent to me that we have been put on the back burner. Time is passing and the Secaucus Police Department detective tells me the car is about to be released to the owner's insurance company. It may then be totaled out and destroyed. Evidence may be lost forever. Finally I call the attorney's office in New York and leave word that he has been discharged from further representation. I follow it up with a certified letter.

A week later I get a copy of a belated investigation report purportedly done by his investigator, and a bill. The report provides little information not already contained in the police reports. I pay the bill and decide it is a small price to pay for no longer being represented by this attorney. Another bitter lesson learned.

Next I decide to contact the president of the Oregon

Trial Lawyers' Association, hopeful he will know someone in New York who can be trusted to handle the case on a long-distance basis. He gives me the name of an attorney he personally knows and who he says is highly qualified and specializes in wrongful death cases such as this. I intend to telephone the attorney the next day.

Before I have an opportunity to call the new lawyer, however, Linnette and I, by chance, are watching the evening national newscast on TV and we see a lawyer being led out of his office in handcuffs, charged with being part of a scheme to defraud insurance companies in bogus injury cases. It is the same lawyer who has been recommended to us. We have dodged another bullet, but we're back where we started.

I am now so discouraged at the thought of working with an out-of-state lawyer, I decide to use a local lawyer who I can oversee and let him or her associate with someone back east. I recall that Bob, who shares an office with me, has used a trial lawyer in downtown Portland on occasion for subrogation work and was very satisfied with him. I had met him, and even though he works for an insurance defense firm, I contact him and arrange to consult with him. He runs a conflicts check to make sure his firm has not represented any of the insurance companies or other parties potentially involved which would ethically prohibit him from talking with us about the case. He tells me he is clear to talk with me. His name is Michael Gentry.

We meet in his office and I show him the various documents I have. We have a long discussion, and he is both sympathetic and objective in his approach, which I appreciate. He seems exactly what we need. A contingent fee agreement is signed, and he undertakes our representation.

It is a great relief, especially to me, to have this burden taken from my shoulders. There are painful details in the legal process that require us to reopen old wounds. Once again, however, a person comes into our lives at a critical time as a relative stranger and performs, as did Henry Mack in New Jersey, with consummate professionalism and kindness for which we are forever grateful. Again, the kindness of strangers.

Over the next few months Mike aggressively pursues the case. Within several months, following the filing of a wrongful death action against James Kiefner, the case is settled with his insurance company for the policy limits. We then negotiate a settlement with our own insurance company on the basis of the fact that Kiefner was underinsured. The settlements are blood money. They do not bring our daughter back. But we are grateful to get these issues resolved and behind us. It is another example of our sense of parenting after death. We can now attend to the more important work of dealing with our own emotional issues as well as those of our surviving children.

DREAMS

AND SO YOU DREAM OF DEATH, AND IN YOUR DREAM you hold her loss in your hands. You turn it first one way and then the other. It is always the same. Death never changes. But then you waken, the air still with her leaving, the room still dying around you, terminal and strong.

CHAPTER
TWENTY-THREE

INCREASINGLY WE DISCOVER HOW ISOLATED WE HAVE BECOME at times. While family stays supportive and close and we grieve together, we find it is often difficult for others to approach us.

Some friends stay close and simply offer their presence without feeling any great need to somehow try to rationalize for us what has happened. Others, however, seem to feel a need to offer platitudes as if they are wisdom. We have come to treasure those who are simply there, who stop by to sit with us for a while, who may even drop off a hot dish or some flowers from time to time. We have yet to hear any rationalization, religious or otherwise, that justifies what has been taken from us, or from Allison. But we try our best to be grateful for what comes our way as we sense how difficult it can be for others who can only imagine what we are experiencing. There are limits, however.

One shirttail relative takes me aside one day and assures

me that Allison died because God wanted another angel and she was so pretty he chose her. I have heard that one many times in recent weeks. Knowing he too has a daughter, I tell him I sincerely hope his daughter will be the next to be given such an honor. That I know what an honor it will be for him if she were to die and become one of God's angels. He gives me a sudden and startled look and, without another word, shuffles away. Perhaps it finally dawns on him how insensitive and stupid his comments are. But I doubt it. I'm not sure what kind of God such folks believe in, but I find it difficult to accept the notion of a God who kills attractive young women just to satisfy his need to be surrounded by pretty angels. To me that sounds more like a maniacal serial killer than a loving heavenly father.

In short, there are no words of "wisdom" that justify the death of one's child. What we learn is that what happens can happen. We have no control over where life takes us and that lives, including our own and those of the ones we love, are fragile at best. What and who is here today may not be here tomorrow. What we have learned is that each of us has a contract at birth with those we love and who love us that either we will witness their deaths, or they will witness ours. It is part of what love is. What, if anything, lies beyond is to me s profound mystery. But we do our best to realize and understand that no one is intentionally trying to be cruel or thoughtless. Each person brings his or her own limitations to the process of grief. Including ourselves. But it's not easy and often serves to make our grieving that much more difficult at times.

Oddly enough we find that some previously close friends have now turned away from us, even as others, not so close, come closer. Longtime friends with whom we had shared many family experiences over the years, virtually disappear from our lives. I suspect they just don't know how to deal with the loss. We understand that, but feel that it is cowardly nonetheless, given the length of the relationships. At the same time, others with whom we have not been especially close in the past have become closer in recent days and have been willing to go on despite our long faces and teary red eyes.

As I return to my law practice I also discover that my professional life is different. A number of my clients, despite their own legal issues and tribulations, come forward to console me, for which I am grateful. Some clients are even able and willing to break through the professional barrier between client and attorney to offer their support on a more personal basis. Normally I would discourage that breakdown of professional barriers, but under these circumstances I do not, and again, I appreciate them.

My relationship with many of my lawyer colleagues, however, is a different matter. I find that for many I seem a marked man. I walk down the corridors of the courthouse, familiar territory for me, and I see lawyers I know coming towards me who then suddenly turn away, seemingly so as to avoid coming in direct contact with me, not knowing what to say to me or how to greet me. Or I sit in the courthouse cafeteria drinking a cup of coffee after a hearing or a trial, and I find myself sitting alone, whereas before there might be a group of us exchanging war stories. Again, I sense they just don't know what to say or how to approach me. I still have that dark cloud hanging over my head, like a character from an old Al Capp cartoon.

However, again, some react differently. One judge,

in particular, invites me into his chambers after a brief
ex-parte appearance in his courtroom, and we talk for
about a half hour or more. He questions me closely about
what happened and about Allison and seems unafraid to
face the reality of the loss and offers his condolences and
best wishes. I have known him for many years, dating
back to when we both worked in the courthouse, he in
the district attorney's office and I, for the civil service
commission, but we were never close friends. We are now.

Linnette has support from her colleagues at the school.
One fellow teacher has also lost a child in an auto accident, a teenage son, just months before Allison's death.
She knows what Linnette is experiencing and how difficult it is for her, and the two of them support each other.
She refers Linnette and me to a support group she attends
called Compassionate Friends.

Compassionate Friends is an organization composed
of bereaved parents who meet periodically. They provide an opportunity for bereaved parents to interact with
others in the same situation. We attend for the first time
about six weeks after Allison's death. Before that we met
on several occasions with a grief counselor at Kaiser Permanente, and Linnette has continued to see her and a
psychiatrist as well.

We attend several of the monthly meetings of the
Friends but eventually decide it is not the best approach
for dealing with grief for us. We find many who partici-
pate do not, in our opinion, seem to be progressing toward
any kind of real healing or emotional evolution. Rather
they seem to be locked into their grief in ways that gives
us the impression they have somehow come to dedicate
their lives to the tragedy, even years later in some cases,

rather than to finally moving on with their lives. Even parents whose children died years and years before seem still as raw as we are in their emotions.

We decided early on that we do not want the wreckage from Allison's death to become a permanent memorial that ultimately destroys us and destroys what the future has to offer us and what we have to offer the future. We do not believe that is something she would have wanted to happen. That is, at least, something we can control.

The organization has obviously served the needs of many over the years. We determined, for various reasons, it is not best for us. We feel the need to either be with folks who are relatively whole and intact, or alone by ourselves.

We are considering looking for a cabin in the woods and have talked about it a great deal. We hope that we will over time in solitude and reflection put our lives back together again. That we have stumbled through thus far and yet made decisions that seem beneficial for us over time is a miracle in itself. There is no guidebook written in stone.

"It's okay. I'm all right."

CHAPTER
TWENTY-FOUR

By August we come to the realization that we need some means to get away from the house, at least on the weekends, and to begin building a new history for ourselves. Not one that excludes Allison, but one that begins to incorporate her death into our new lives. Our recent journey around the Pacific Northwest gave us such a reprieve. But at home, the house is both just a home for us and a place of torture at times, a place where she continues to live and where we still, at times, hear her moving about, getting on with her life. We decide we need someplace where we can go where she has never been. We need some sense of a neutral ground.

As the end of summer nears we decide to try to buy that small cabin somewhere, some place where we can get away but that is still close. The foothills of Mt. Hood seem a logical choice. It is an easy drive from where we live. And so we begin our search. We approach a realtor in the Hoodland area, Liz Warren, and she begins showing us various cabins that are on the market. All of them, however, are sunk deep into the forest and lost in shadow for much of the time. To us they look depressing and dismal. We want something out in the open and accessible to sunlight. We are beginning to get discouraged and wonder if it is such a good idea after all.

But then one day Liz takes us to see a small cabin near Rhododendron, about a mile south of the highway, between the Zigzag River and Still Creek. We park in an open area surrounded by slender lodge pole pine and follow a narrow curved path to where the cabin sits. We can see its outline through the tall, delicate trees, trees more reminiscent of Central Oregon than Western. And then suddenly, as we turn the final bend in the path, there it is, bathed in sunlight, its steep, pitched roof and high front wall of glass windows reaching to the eaves greeting us.

After showing us through the interior, we decide to make an offer that, with some negotiation, is accepted. Later we learn the seller, Anne Bentley, a retired school art teacher, bought this little cabin years ago soon after the death of her own daughter, an only child. She came up to this cabin in the woods to rebuild her life. We must have been led to this place and to this person. Yet another encounter with the lives of strangers.

The purchase closes by the end of summer, and we find ourselves now the owners of this small cabin lost in the forest between a rushing dynamo of a river careening down the mountainside in one direction and a quiet, gently flowing creek in the other direction. We come to this place virtually every weekend. We leave town immediately after we get home from work late on a Friday afternoon, grab our small backpacks, packed and ready for us, and it takes less than an hour of driving to get to the cabin. We stow our gear and groceries, build a fire in the old wood stove to begin warming the cabin, and go a local restaurant, usually the Alpine Hut or the Log Lodge in Rhododendron for a dinner of burgers and fries. Maybe a gin and tonic. For sure a gin and tonic. Then we return to Portland late Sunday afternoon. Two days and two nights at the cabin can feel like forever.

Here, deep in this forest of tall pines and mountain laurel, with the river and creek always just steps away, we introduce ourselves to our new world. We walk and hike along the river, follow sections of the Barlow Trail, nearly lost in the dense foliage, the route taken to Oregon by Linnette's ancestors, climb Flag Mountain to stand silent on its eastern edge looking out toward the steep flanks of Mt. Hood, and then, at end of day, return to the warmth of the cabin to spend an evening watching the fire in the big, stone fireplace, reading or talking. A place of refuge. A place my mother, with her Scottish brogue, would come to call "The Wee Housie."

TIME TRAVEL

WE ARE ON OUR WAY TO SPAIN AND PORTUGAL. WE have stopped over in New York City for a couple of nights as the flight to Lisbon was full and, flying standby, we could not get on. And so we are waiting for the next flight out to Lisbon. We have flown from Portland on TWA, guests of Allison, who is a flight attendant for the airline, and we are flying first class. We are intending to fly to Lisbon and then join a land tour and end up in Madrid and fly home from there, through J.F.Kennedy.

While we are in New York City waiting to get out, we are guests of Allison's employers, the Rapaport family, a family of orthodox Jews. Allison and her friend Suzanne are working as nannies for the family that, at this time, has six children, all boys except the youngest, a little girl named Miriam. Suzanne works for them full time and Allison between flights out for TWA. The parents, it seems, have a child each year.

The family lives in an apartment in the heart of this huge city. It is a large apartment on the seventh and eighth floors, as they have recently obtained the apartment directly above them, and have now connected the two with a winding stairway, doubling their living space. The children play in an enclosed playground behind the building. There is no grass, but there are a few playground structures, swings and a slide. The father is a diamond broker and the mother works with him.

Because we have not been able to catch our flight out of the country, they have graciously invited us to stay with them. We have never been in an orthodox Jewish home before. They keep a kosher kitchen, and observe many rituals and rules with which we are unfamiliar. Allison has been with them now for several months and has learned the ropes, so she is able to guide us to avoid missteps. They are very kind to us and we feel welcome. I tell them of my own Jewish family history, what little I know, and they are most interested and give me some information on how I might pursue more knowledge of the family history.

Their children have names like Slomo and Slimie, and, like all little boys, especially ones cooped up in a tall apartment building in the middle of a gigantic, bustling city, are restless and anxious to make a break for it at any time. Allison loves children and did a great deal of babysitting in Portland when she was in high school. She is a bit crazy and freewheeling and the kids love her.

One afternoon we decide to take the boys, along with Miriam, out for a walk, perhaps to a *nearby park and for pizza. We follow along as Allison herds the entire bunch out onto the sidewalk, and we chase them all down the street, the kids hooting and hollering and Allison doing the same. We can hardly keep up. I have this sudden vision of Allison, 10 or 20 years from now, herding her own children, our grandchildren, to the park to play. She will be laughing. They will be laughing.*

"It's okay. I'm all right."

CHAPTER TWENTY-SIX

WE HAVE MADE IT THROUGH SUMMER AND THE PARADE OF "special days," --- birthdays, occasions honoring parenthood, the various summer events that have become special in our family over the years, such as trips to the Kittrell beach cabin or camping trips. And now the fall season is upon us and, soon we'll be facing winter. For Linnette that means returning to the classroom. For me a more intense caseload as clients return from summer vacations. I have urged her to reconsider taking a leave of absence for up to a year or, perhaps, even early retirement. But she will have none of that.

Summer has been a mixed bag. We had the lovely trip into Montana and beyond, and that did us immense good. We had Aaron home for the summer, and that was good, but he will soon be leaving for his next year at the University of Washington. The house will be so quiet once again. Deathly so. My mother had her birthday in early August and Linnette and I had our wedding anniversary a few days ago. It was difficult to work up much enthusiasm for either.

But soon the weather will begin its change from sunshine and blue skies to the steady drizzle and grayness of an Oregon winter. The purchase of the little cabin, that has come to now be called "The Bleeding Place," will help. We have been going up there every weekend, and sometimes during the week too, when I can get away. We are getting to know the Mt. Hood foothills, hiking the trails, investigating the nooks and crannies of the forest, and often sit by ourselves on the old Still Creek Bridge, just watching the creek flow down off Mt. Hood until it merges into the Zigzag River downstream. The salmon are now returning home from the sea and we watch for hours as they struggle up the creek to their spawning grounds, their bodies appearing black and bruised, beating themselves on the rocks as they leap from eddy to eddy.

In the evening it is off to the Alpine Hut or the Log Lodge for dinner, a quiet dinner, along with a drink of something to pacify us. Then it is back to the cabin to sit in the dark in front of the fireplace, with the outside spotlight turned on, and talk, or sit and just be alone. Sometimes our best conversations are silence. Just the three of us. Then it's off to bed.

Gradually, past Labor Day, again there are the old obligations. I know it will soon be October, and then November. Another round of holidays for which I will never be quite ready. Both of us worry about Aaron, as he is not one to express his feelings easily. Jennifer has Ben to stand by her side. She is preparing for her career as a social worker and I trust her to understand her emotions and her own unique connections to Allison, connections

I will never entirely understand or know. Aaron too had his own special relationship with Allison, and I worry that he may not be as capable at this point in his life to work through what has happened. And being away at school, away from his parents, may make that even more difficult. The dynamics of the relationship of siblings is considerably different than that of parent and child. I are concerned that I not only may not understand those differences well enough, but also that I may have so little of myself to give to understand it.

The days have a chill in the air. I went to retrieve the newspaper this morning and as I was returning to the house I heard above me a frantic honking and honking. I looked up and the sky was filled with geese, vast "V's" of them, flying south. I just stood in wonder. In such brief moments there are more lessons of grief: salmon struggling against the flow of the stream to spawn. Geese heading south for the winter, flying hundreds, if not thousands of miles. The optimism of nature. I feel a part of something far more intricate and special than I would have otherwise imagined. Whether we are ready or not, the world takes us with it. Whatever happens, happens. We have so little control. I learn to live my new life by going where I have to go.

THE SOURCE

THE HOUSE IS SO QUIET. IT IS NIGHTTIME. AARON HAS returned to Seattle. It is just the two of us. Or is it? We are never quite certain. As night falls we hear again the sounds that emanate from the darkness. Our saner selves know it is not so. Our in-saners selves aren't so sure. We have learned to accept what comes to us. We struggle to rebuild our lives. To accept what keeps us intact. Even if it is an illusion. We are no longer bound by the laws of physics. It is not a matter of religion with us. It is a matter of what keeps us going. How we are able to accept the reality of our lives one more day. This is the process by which our child becomes us. The process by which she slowly returns to the source.

CHAPTER TWENTY-SIX

THE FLAG MOUNTAIN TRAIL IN THE FOOTHILLS OF MT. HOOD begins just off Rd. 20 E. At first it is a gentle meandering path through lovely old growth. Then it begins its ascent with switchbacks zigzagging their way up the side of its steep rocky face. As one climbs higher the view of Mt. Hood to the east becomes more evident as the trees thin out and the vista opens up. From the very top of the ridge the trail leads again into old growth forest.

Linnette and I, as usual, are up at the cabin for another weekend taking advantage of the late summer, early fall weather and a time to be alone together following a busy work-week apart. Perhaps a last chance to hike Flag Mountain before winter sets in. We each have a small backpack with water, a snack to eat on the trail, and a flashlight. I have my camera.

At the top we stand for a few moments, contemplating the grandeur of Mt. Hood on the far eastern horizon, but so close we think we can almost touch it, its flanks still covered in old snow, despite the fact that it is so early in the season and there has been no new snowfall since last winter. We can even see the vertical tracks left by summer skiers. I sit on a rock and take some photos while Linnette forages for interesting pinecones, arrowheads, or other memorabilia to take back to the cabin. It's a good excuse to rest from the climb.

From here the trail continues fairly level and winds its way across the flat top of Flag Mountain to its southern slope. There the descent begins, switch-backing down the other side ending with the Still Creek Road, which connects the lower foothills to Trillium Lake, and across the road to Still Creek itself, where the creek slides down off the mountain to meet up with the Zigzag River farther downstream. The hike has taken about two hours.

There are fishermen camped by Still Creek, perhaps a half dozen, all men, and they ignore us as they go about their efforts to land a fish, wading hip deep in the stream, which here widens and acts more like a river, eddies swirling around their legs as they brace themselves to cast their lines out one after the other. We watch for a while, eat our snacks, and then prepare to begin our return trip up across the mountain and back to the cabin. It is a warm day despite the occasional chill in the air that tells us winter is on its way. The trail here is open to the sky with few trees to protect us, and the late afternoon sun beats down on us. Soon, however, we reenter old growth and it cools quickly, as we lose ourselves in the shadows of tall pine. Mountain Laurel is everywhere. The odor of pine and Douglas fir is intense and the soft feel of needles crackling beneath our hiking boots is oddly comforting.

These moments are the reason we come here. We

are alone. We have not encountered another person on the trail except us. But for the fishermen now far behind us, there has been no one. We hear occasional crashing sounds in the denseness of the forest from time to time. We have seen signs of bear on some of the trees, and scat from deer. But we have not seen the creatures themselves. They remain hidden. Only the occasional chipmunk or Douglas squirrel darting about and offering complaints.

Once more we reach the vista point where we can again stare up at the broad face of Mt. Hood and can again marvel at its majesty. Then suddenly Linnette points up to two bald eagles circling slowly overhead, searching for signs of dinner below. They drop down to check us out. They glide around and around, riding the air currents until they are just about twenty-five or thirty feet above us, wingspans at least six feet across. Then they suddenly reverse course and once again swoop upward and away, satisfied we are not the meal they had hoped for. Linnette and I watch in awe.

And then we see it. Floating gently down to us, a lone eagle feather, a gift from one of our wild friends. I am reminded of the Indian legend that tells us that the two-toned eagle feather is sacred and represents light and dark, summer and winter, peace and war, and, finally, life and death. It is the story of our own lives floating down to us.

CHAPTER
TWENTY-SEVEN

TODAY IS THE FIRST OF OCTOBER. IT HAS BEEN ALMOST SEVEN months now. Linnette stills drags herself off to work. I still go to the office every weekday morning, or off to a courthouse somewhere to make a court appearance. The days seem to run together. If it were not for the promise of weekends and the cabin, I don't think we could make it through. But we have now reached the point where we often seem to be moving on different tracks. We no longer function simply as a bereaved couple, clutching desperately to one another. We have regained a sense of individual existence through this process of grieving. There are those days when Linnette might appear to me to be feeling better, and I don't. Or vice versa. I suppose this is good, but at the same time, it feels like we are often at odds. We can each become so lost in our own sense of despair it is hard to reach out to the other person, or to understand how each of us can be different in how and what we are feeling and when.

The physical pain that ripped through my body when I first learned of Allison's death abated over a matter of several weeks and was replaced first by numbness and then, eventually by an almost constant aching.

Linnette is getting professional help. I could probably use it too but, other than a couple of sessions with a social worker at Kaiser along with Linnette and the kids, I have not. I seek help from reading the literature of grief. I'm not sure why I have resisted counseling. Perhaps it is fear. Perhaps it is that I don't want to admit I need it. That I am as needy as I seem to be. In some respects, Linnette seems stronger than I am. She seems to have a better sense of what she needs to do to get through this. I muddle forward, thinking somehow work alone will do it. But I get no enjoyment from the work. The office or the courtroom is just a place to be. There is no excitement. No zest. Except for the pro bono work, and that is not enough. That only heightens my sense of despair, knowing it won't earn me a livelihood.

We go up to the cemetery but not as often. Perhaps it is the change in the weather that deters us. Standing there on that hillside in the rain is more depressing than not going. I may have reached the point where I know there is nothing that is going to be accomplished by our being there. Nothing will change. Our parenting has come to naught. What is still is. Instead we sit around the house in the evenings, sometimes reading, sometimes watching TV, sometimes just trying to get as far away from one another as we can, Linnette in the bedroom upstairs, me downstairs in the family room. Not in anger so much as a need to be alone, to be separate. Little by little, as the days pass, we seem to be going in different directions.

But, thankfully, there are still the weekends at the cabin. I live for these weekends. We return to the cabin every Friday evening, desperate for the solitude of the mountain, that sense of once again being closed off from the outside world with the dense forest all around us, the sounds of the river not far away, and the dark silence of the trees. It is here that we reconnect. It is here that we become a couple again, even if we sometimes seem lost in our own thoughts.

Now it is evening, and I am sitting in front of the huge stone fireplace, gently smoking my pipe, an old briar that once belonged to my Scottish grandfather, watching the flames lick the fresh logs of fir and pine, the occasional crackling sound of pitch. The chimney does not draw well and wispy plumes of smoke drift from the fireplace and join with the smoke from the old briar. We have recently replaced the ancient trash burner with a new wood-burning pellet stove, and it sits where the burner sat, sending its heat to all corners of the small cabin. It is much more efficient and much safer. We have installed an electric baseboard heater in the back bedroom and in the bathroom, but otherwise the wood stove and the fireplace heat the cabin. The wall on the south side of the living room is all glass. As night falls I turn on the outside spotlight and we sit for hours looking out into the darkness that surrounds us beyond the reach of the long fingers of light. I am reading a book, *Meetings at the Edge*, by Stephen Levine. Linnette is just watching the fire in the fireplace burn down. Finally I stoke up the pellet stove so it will last until morning. Then we go to bed, ready to start the night shift.

Here we find healing to be a twenty-four-hour job.

THE LOST DAUGHTER

DAUGHTER, IT COULD BE YESTERDAY, APRIL 8TH. THE year is always now. However we live hardens, sets its path, shows us the way. Even now we see the crash, your body broken, lying by that freeway in New Jersey. Rain, then darkness, did for you what we could not. We hope within that violence there was peace, a moment when you lifted up and the pain was gone. Daughter, in the midst of death we still reach out, we, the children you will never have, you, the parent of our grieving.

CHAPTER
TWENTY-SEVEN

IT IS THE LONG THANKSGIVING WEEKEND, OUR FIRST MAJOR family holiday without Allison. Aaron is home from university, with his girlfriend, Barbara, a fellow student, who, it turns out, will later become our daughter-in-law, although we don't know it at the time. Jennifer and our son-in-law Ben are with us too. We are all at the cabin. It is a full house. The little place is maxed out. The young folk are all going up to Timberline to ski. Linnette will go with them, but I stay at the cabin to get it warmed up.

We got here early in the day, driving through a heavy snowfall, the earliest snowfall we have yet seen at this elevation. Not having chains on the car and being fully unprepared, we got stuck in our own driveway coming in off the highway. We called the local towing company and for cash on the line they agreed to come and pull us out of the deep drift we had slid into. The husky woman driving the tow truck looked at us like we were the most pathetic greenhorns she had ever seen. I sensed somehow she had seen quite a few. With the others now gone farther up the mountain, I tend to the cabin, firing up the pellet stove and the fireplace. By the time the others arrive back it is warm and inviting.

With skiing over for the day, hungry, we all head down to the Resort at the Mountain at Bowman's for their buffet Thanksgiving dinner. Linnette has no desire to cook a huge meal and put out the usual Thanksgiving spread. The lodge is decorated for the season, and folks are milling around. Somehow being lost in the crowd works magic for me. We are ushered to a long table that had been reserved for us in one of the far rooms and are given instructions how to navigate the buffet tables spread out at the other end of the room. It is "all you can eat" and the young folks, famished from skiing, take full advantage. With plates heaped high, we all reconvene and begin eating and drinking in celebration of the season, both Thanksgiving and the beginning of the Christmas holidays. Already there are carolers wandering about from room to room, singing Christmas songs.

All the while, seated with us but invisible to those around us is Allison. Again we celebrate a special event in her absence. First it was Mother's Day, then family birthdays, then Father's Day. Now this. Last night Linnette and I lay in our bed at home and listened once again to the night music of her past life echoing through the bedroom wall from her room. But here now at the lodge we are just another family, like all the others around us, as we struggle to make things normal when they are not. With each bite of the sumptuous food I think of the one who is not here. Little by little our talk brings her into the scene. Having Barbara and Ben with us helps extend our sense of family.

With dinner over we return to the cabin, which greets us with its warmth, like a tiny glowing friend sitting in the descending dusk waiting for us with the snow falling all around it and the windows lit and welcoming. In the short time we have owned this place it has proven its worth. We spend the balance of the day just watching the deep shadows settle into the forest, the outside spotlight turned on to illuminate the snowfall and the tree limbs bent down and graced with white. We sit together around the fireplace, drinking wine and cider and talking, mostly about Allison and what adventures she would be having if she were alive and traveling the world. We imitate her squeaky voice and laugh. We tell Allison stories until it is finally time to get some sleep. Linnette and I retire to our tiny back bedroom. Jennifer and Ben climb up the ladder to the sleeping loft and Aaron and Barb sack out in the living room in sleeping bags laid out on the floor in front of the fireplace.

About midnight I wake up and quietly tiptoe into the kitchen area for a glass of water, and can see the two sleeping mounds on the living room floor breathing gently, up and down, and can hear the sounds of sleep floating down from the loft above. The fire in the fireplace has died away to embers and ash, just glowing there in the dark. It seems the walls of the little cabin emanate with new life. Here, for this brief time, we are a family again. A family almost whole. Almost complete. Almost.

CHAPTER
TWENTY-EIGHT

With the Thanksgiving holiday over Aaron returns to Seattle and Jenn returns to grad school at PSU. The Christmas holidays are now in full force, lights twinkling, flocked evergreen trees, decorations up in the heart of the city, Christmas music everywhere. I begin to feel overwhelmed. The holiday season is always difficult in law practice anyway because so many custody and visitation issues arise. Divorced and separated parents are squabbling over who gets the children for the holidays and when and how much support should be paid, and on and on. It seems any excuse to fight over the children comes to the surface of broken relationships at this time of year. The fights seem to intensify during the Christmas holidays. The gift that keeps on giving. For Linnette it means her class of second graders is getting more and more excited, and the school is in the throes of preparing special programs for parents and grandparents to attend.

For me, all of this goes against the grain of where I am emotionally. I don't want to deprive others of their joy but I can't put my heart in it. I find myself resenting my clients and their spouses or ex-spouses who are often needlessly, in my view, fighting over access to their children when all I can think of is that I have lost mine. It drains me of the necessary fire to invest myself in their cases, although I'm not sure I fully realize that. It is another example of the extent of my disability. At times I seem to be feeling so sorry for myself I can't really evaluate the world around me, including the needs of my clients.

We head to the cabin every weekend to get away. Late on Friday afternoon, as soon as we get home from work we throw our packs into the car and begin our drive up the mountain. The snow on the ground is sometimes so deep we can't drive in all the way and must park on the highway and hike in with our provisions for the weekend on our backs. It is a little over a mile. One weekend the snow was almost hip deep. There is something eerie about hiking in through the snow as it is getting dark and the dense forest is all around us, drawing us in. Sounds are magnified and the shadows deepen. And then, suddenly, there it is, the little cabin, waiting for us. I fire up the pellet stove and fireplace and we huddle together on the sofa until it has warmed up enough to settle in.

In better weather we would leave and go back to the highway and have dinner at one of the restaurants, letting the cabin warm up. But now, with the snow so deep, we can't do that. But the little place warms quickly, and we have a simple dinner, a couple of drinks, and go to bed early. On Saturday and Sunday we read, talk and hike into the woods, up the road to the Zigzag River as far as we can go, and enjoy the solitude. About a quarter mile up Road 20 is a small stretch of what was decades ago part of the old Barlow Trail, which is the last portion of the Oregon Trail that brought the early settlers into the Willamette Valley. We walk along the remnants of the trail, through the snow and I think back on all those pioneers who wearily trudged through here in the 1800s, including Linnette's relatives. It gives me a sense of connection to a time long past, a feel for being part of a history, of family.

By late Sunday afternoon we are again on the road going home. Back to reality. Back to the world we have to learn to be a part of once again. I know we can't stay at the cabin forever. While it is a refuge, it is not the only world we inhabit. Linnette returns to school. I return to the office and those barking dogs. Back to the decorations and the seasonal music, the crowded shopping malls and the replay of traditional holiday productions on television, with their sunny messages of lives renewed and reborn. I don't feel exactly like Scrooge, but I'm not part of the Season either. I know the day is coming, and it is hard to know what my feelings are. There is shopping to be done even if I don't feel like doing it. There are family plans to be made, even if I don't feel like making them.

Soon school is out for Linnette and she will have a couple of weeks without having to head off to work each day. But still she has this holiday to deal with, which may be worse. I am busier than ever at the office, with hearings, one after the other. To some extent, it takes my mind off my own ills for a while. But it is a false reprieve.

Finally Christmas day dawns, after a quiet Christmas Eve, and we do what we have to do to get through it and nothing more. Aaron is a Christmas Eve baby and we celebrated his birthday as best we could. The week between Christmas and New Years is quiet and my time at the office is limited. Come the new year, however, the bankruptcies will come storming in, as all those folks who overspent during the holidays will discover their credit cards are maxed out and they are unable to pay their bills. This will be followed by divorces, as the stress of the holidays and the delinquent bills overtake some couples and will prove to be the final blow. This heightens my sense of living off the woes of others.

Linnette heads back to school with the turning of the year, and I prepare for the onslaught of new business. Grist for the lawyer's mill. With the changing of the calendar I am again mindful of how time is passing and Allison is becoming history whether we want her to or not. She died not this year, but last year. And then there will be another, and another. The years will build up and we will be further removed from her life as time passes. Another lesson of grief: Time passes. There is nothing we can do about it.

CHAPTER
TWENTY-NINE

In the mid-1840s and beyond wagons trains of early settlers to the Oregon Territory snaked their way along the Barlow Trail toward Oregon City, along the western flanks of Mt. Hood, a trail that was slow and treacherous. One such wagon train in 1848 stopped at the meadows, high in the foothills of Mt. Hood to winter as the remainder of the trail plummeted down the mountainside and it was necessary to wait out winter in order to navigate it safely and successfully

.A newborn baby girl was the newest member of that wagon train. Her mother had died earlier on the trail giving birth to her. The mother was buried in a now unknown gravesite, unmarked and lost to time. The baby girl, who had also not yet been named, died an accidental death while the pioneers were encamped on Mt. Hood, not far from the cabin.

Today a grave marker labeled only "Baby Morgan" is

still visible on the edge of that meadow, known as Summit Meadows, a stone with a plaque marking the spot where she lies. As we continue to hike and explore the mountain that has become our salvation, we stop often as we hike by the meadow, to contemplate that young life that came and went so soon. A child who did not live enough days to even acquire a name. A child who had no life beyond the first days of infancy.

A child who would have been all but forgotten. Except in the minds and hearts of her immediate family, as the wagon train moved on and left the mountainside with the advent of spring, and moved down toward the lowlands, on to its destination and dispersed. There the survivors made their land claims in the Willamette Valley, cleared the land, cultivated their farms, started their businesses, built their schools, and made a new life for themselves.

But Baby Girl Morgan was not forgotten. Her father remembered her. And his descendants have as well. Each late summer, so we are told, the descendants of Baby Girl Morgan gather at the gravesite of this tiny speck of life that disappeared so quickly and remember her with a picnic and festivities.

While her mother lies in an unknown, unmarked grave, the child she gave life to still lives on in the lives of her descendants. We are told her family, to this very day, visit annually to celebrate that tiny life. And we who also honor that brief life gather too. Yet another grave site of one gone too soon.

CHAPTER THIRTY

WINTER SETTLES IN ON US. JANUARY, THEN FEBRUARY. WHEN we are at the cabin winter can be a lovely time of solitude and reflection. We feel we are sealed into our own little world and can fashion it to meet our needs. But at home in the city, winter is just a time of rain, occasional snow and slush, and grayness, both inside and out.

I go to work and I come home. Going to the cemetery is usually a drive after work across town through the rain and rush hour traffic and then a short hike down the hill from the parking lot through the wet and sodden grass. The gravesite looks lost and forlorn. The trees are bare and the cemetery grounds often windswept and empty of life. We do not go daily as we did for a long time, but still go several times a week. We leave flowers but they appear stark and out of place sitting upright in the brass urn with the rain pouring down.

On the rare sunny day, I stand mute for a while and then hold onto Linnette. On other days we stay only briefly and then race back to the car. Since it is usually late in the day, we stop at Cassidy's on our way home for a light dinner and a couple of drinks. Always we are the odd couple sitting off in a dark corner of the bar feeling sorry for ourselves. The waitresses have come to know us. They cut us some slack.

I find my law practice to be increasingly repetitive and unrewarding. I feel like I am going around in circles, like the proverbial record, being replayed over and over. Each new client looks the same to me as the last. I have heard all the same questions asked, the same tales of woe. I give the same answers over and over. I have no sense of emotional investment in my work. All the emotion I have to spend is spent on myself and Linnette. I have nothing left for clients. I move through each workday in a fog. Were it not for the need to earn a living, I would not be in the office. At times I question my own sanity.

There has been one bright spot. I have been doing pro bono work with the Multnomah Bar Volunteer Lawyer Project that operates free legal clinics for low-income clients throughout the county. I have been helping to staff the clinics, usually about once a week.

There I meet with clients referred by the Project who are, by any standard, worse off then I am. Caught up in eviction proceedings, benefits entanglements, used car contracts and bankruptcies, they are all in one way or another living life on the edge. They lack the means to deal with the issues that are impacting and shaping their lives. Somehow, knowing that they could not otherwise afford an attorney or representation energizes me and allows me to focus in a way that is otherwise missing from my fee-generating practice. They are desperate, and I know if I don't help them it is not likely that anyone will. Their desperation feeds my needs and overcomes my sense of self. I realize they are helping me as much as I am helping them. In a sense we are using each other. As a result, I find myself drawn more and more to the work in the clinics.

Doing the pro bono work is a great help to me personally, but it does not pay the bills. I have to keep bringing in enough in fees to keep the doors open and take something home. Linnette and I may almost be empty nesters, but we are not there quite yet, and even empty nesters have to eat and make mortgage payments. I feel caught in a trap from which there seems no escape.

As March approaches we are both dreading it. Allison's first birthday since her death. Normally I would be looking forward to spring, the changing weather, the warming temperatures, a few sunny days. But not this year. While I long to have the weather change to warmer, dryer days, I find the movement of time inexorably toward the 12th of March, her birthday, filling me with increased anxiety.

I recall now how sweet the buildup to her birthday was last year; how she had been on leave from the airline for medical reasons and was staying with us, and how our days were filled with just sitting around with her, Allison in her old pink bathrobe, just chatting and getting caught up on her life, her loves and her adventures. For her birthday we gave her an emerald ring. It was to be our last gift to her. Sometimes I wish we had known that. Other times, no, it would have been too painful to endure. If what ultimately happened had to happen, it was better that we were all able to enjoy those few weeks of sweet togetherness unencumbered by the future. For now, I just mark the days off on the calendar and wait. The twisted emerald ring lies in its manila envelope along with the other items found at the scene of her accident.

FLYING STANDBY

WE ARE SOMEWHERE OVER THE ATLANTIC, NEW York to Madrid, 35,000 ft., flying standby. TWA Flt. 967. We had hoped to board the plane to Lisbon, but it was full, and rather than wait two more days for the next one, we decided to get on this flight to Madrid. We will catch a TAP flight from there to Lisbon and hopefully catch up with our luggage. The upside of all this is that Allison is part of the flight crew and we are, for the first time, seeing her in action. It is the "Amazing Allison" again, moving with ease about the cabin, attending to the needs of passengers, calming crying children, serving food and drink. She is enjoying entertaining us. She just celebrated her twenty-first birthday in Paris on a layover. The crew took her nightclubbing to the Moulin Rouge. All she needs now is her tall hat, the black cape and her magic wand. I expect her to find a nickel behind my ear.

CHAPTER THIRTY-ONE

ON THIS DATE OF HER BIRTH WE ONCE AGAIN MUST ACKNOWLedge death. On days like this her death hovers over us like a dark hand. The weather is beautiful: clear blue sky, unseasonably cold for this late in winter, a biting east wind. Not the usual dreary drizzle of mid-March. And so we stand here on this cemetery hillside, our feet planted as if we were sturdy, when we are not. The trek down this hillside from the parking lot gets more difficult. Our child, who is forever young, remains as she was. We, on the other hand, slip into grayness. What Robert Frost once described as the "gray disguise of years."

So now we, her parents, stand, side by side, flowers in hand, still here, looking out across the vast expanse of rich, green lawns so neatly maintained, and then down at the now familiar mottled granite plaque with its etched letters, the carved rose, dates that no longer have any meaning to real life.

The world is no longer the world it was. But still, standing here holding each other up against the east wind that buffets us, we long to simply hear again the sound of her voice, to hear again those last words that disappeared so quickly and so finally into the chill of that dark night. *"It's okay. I'm all right."*

The flowers we bought at the Safeway store this morning now struggle to remain upright in their brass urn. They lean their slender stems hard against the incessant blasts of arctic air that come careening at us, funneling down the Columbia River Gorge from Canada. Pink roses. Delicate. Like those we put so carefully on her casket that day in early April almost one year ago. There were light April showers that day when we laid her in this place. It was newly spring and the earth was beginning to warm. Not like today.

With each visit we see how the neighborhood has expanded. Jessica, age five, lies over there, just beneath that great blue spruce tree. There is a balloon (Jessica, we love you! it says) still bobbing and drifting above her gravesite. For a long time there was a stuffed toy, a Scotty dog, moldering in the shadow of her stone, keeping watch.

Twenty feet to the west lies Ting Lee, age 21. His stone is engraved in Asian characters and his mother still visits often, burning tall, thin sticks of incense and stretching her body across his plot, no matter the weather, her arms outstretched to embrace him, chanting and weeping.

Allison's most immediate neighbor, Matt, still occupies his plot of earth not more than ten feet away. He was seventeen when he took up residence here. He will always be seventeen. And now, more recently, on each side of him, Kurt and Marin, his parents, one after the other, have joined him. Matt, like Allison, died in a car crash. It is said that Kurt and Marin may have drunk themselves to death.

And so we accept this March, this birthday. Another day together staring down at the cold, dark earth as if she might suddenly appear before us, whole and real. Still our child. We, still her parents. Still waiting for the rest of her life to somehow begin.

CHAPTER THIRTY-TWO

It is late August. We are standing on the Still Creek Bridge. From this narrow, one-lane, wooden bridge we can survey Still Creek from two perspectives. One to the south, where in spring the waters cascade down off Mt. Hood. The other to the north where the creek will eventually merge with the Zigzag River another mile or two downstream, just below Rhododendron. The view to the south is green and softer at this time of year, the creek now shallow and gentle. Soon, however, salmon will return, struggling up and up from the sea in their long quest for home. They will batter themselves across the rocks that jut from just beneath the surface of the stream as they throw themselves from one eddy to another, over one barrier, then another, their blackened bodies barely still alive.

We come here to the foothills of the Cascades often, and in every season, to see again the best evidence of who we are: Laurel Canyon, Flag Mountain, the marks left of wagons and people heading west on the Barlow

Trail. But especially at this time in late summer as it is where we come to celebrate yet another anniversary and to acknowledge our own time together. Soon it will be fall again. And then winter. Another year without her.

There is a morning chill in the air already. Set against the backdrop of tall firs and pine, the deciduous trees that dip their lower branches over the creek are beginning to shed their leaves into the swirling waters. The vine maples are turning, first a faint yellow and then deepening finally to a flaming orange and red. Together we stand, first on one side of the bridge, looking to the north, and then on the other, looking south. We never vary from this ritual. We never cease to marvel, both at the view and at the fact that we are still here, still together, mother and father, husband and wife, still holding this vision in our hearts of a place on this earth where we are finally at peace. Where the marriage of what the eye sees is complete and whole.

Soon, when the snow falls, and the banks of the creek fill with white and the snow piles onto the rocks and the railings of the bridge, we will again walk down this narrow road, hand in hand. We will again check the spot where only last summer we saw the ghostly white stems of Indian pipe, their now black and dying stalks still visible, rising up out of the drifts. We might see wood ducks swimming against the current, their brilliant colors flashing in the sun.

Then again, like today, we will be alone here, alone with the murmur of the creek, the gentle swirling of water as it slides beneath us, and the sweet scent of old growth.

CHAPTER
THIRTY-THREE

WE HAVE SURVIVED ANOTHER SUMMER AND ARE NOW INTO another fall. October has morphed into November. I continue to make my daily weekday trips to the office or to one of the area courthouses. I continue to meet with clients old and new. I do my best to invest myself in the issues they bring to me. But it's not easy. I look forward to Fridays and our weekend trips to the cabin, our hikes, our time spent on the old Still Creek Bridge just watching Still Creek slide beneath us, and then our walks into town for dinner. The quiet evenings watching the forest disappear into the darkness as the fire in the old stone fireplace burns down.

But then there is inevitably Sunday and the return-drive into town, a return to our so-called "normal lives," which are no longer normal. We walk into the house and the air we breathe thickens in our throats and we take up our lives where we left off the prior Friday. Nothing seems to have changed. What is gone is still gone. Who is gone is still gone.

Monday mornings we wake from the remnants of a restless sleep and slowly take on the new day. Today Linnette prepares for her trip to Gresham and school. I don my lawyer's uniform, my suit and tie, polished shoes. Briefcase in hand I head out the door.

Today I have a hearing in the county courthouse in downtown Portland. It will take up most of the morning. My client is seeking increased visitation rights with his two children following what was a recently contested divorce. It will no doubt get nasty. The closer we get toward the holiday season the more traumatic the domestic relations issues become. December will be the worst. And then in January the divorces and bankruptcies will come flooding in as whatever restraints the holiday season might have imposed will be gone and what was held together by sheer willpower will have dissolved with the season. The high season for lawyers. Unfortunately.

I meet my client, a man in his late thirties, outside the courtroom door and we have a little time to review what we expect, or at least hope, will transpire. He is nervous as a cat. For me it's just another day in the barrel. Opposing counsel and her client arrive and we all enter the court-room together. The judge is ready to begin. And so it goes.

It is close to noon when we emerge, my client having gotten his visitation increased to his satisfaction. The ex-wife is not so happy and she and her attorney leave as quickly as they came. The stage has been set for another Christmas season. The human comedy plays out here daily.

And so goes my week and my month. One hearing after another. Occasionally a full trial. Many hours sitting in my office staring at the certificates on my ego wall. We are slowly edging toward another year. For me, another year without her.

I think back on the pro bono legal clinic I was staffing two weeks ago. An afternoon sitting in a shabby office in a church basement in Gresham interviewing the broken and homeless, the destitute and the down and out. I have been doing that clinic now for several months, as well as the Hispanic Clinic in Old Town and the Urban League Clinic in North Portland. With each clinic I am meeting folks who are desperate for my help.

A Hispanic family bought a used car from a dealership on 82nd Ave. The car broke down within days and it appears, given their lack of English, they were misled as to its condition. An elderly man living in a flophouse in Old Town is being evicted and has nowhere else to go. His landlord has failed to give him proper notice. A young woman, her face badly bruised by an ex-boyfriend needs a restraining order to protect herself and her children. The parade of the destitute keeps coming through my little office, wherever I have managed to set up shop, an old storefront, a spare room at a homeless shelter, a church basement. It is only I, an old desk, a yellow legal pad and whatever solace I can provide. To these folks, I am the lawyer of last resort. If I can't help them, no one else will.

In this work I feel alive once again. They are using me, but I am using them as well. With my usual fee-paying clients, if I don't or can't help them some other lawyer down the street will be happy to earn a fee doing so. But with these clients, I am it. Realistically, there will be no other.

CHAPTER THIRTY-FOUR

IT IS NOW MID-NOVEMBER. TODAY I HAVE BEEN IN COURT IN downtown Portland at a hearing which I had antici-pated would take about an hour. It, in fact, has lasted all morning and into the lunch hour. The judge didn't want to break for lunch as we were so close to the end.

I have agreed to staff a free legal clinic in Old Town, sponsored by the Multnomah County Bar's Volunteer Lawyer Project, and have low-income clients scheduled every half hour from 1 p.m. through the balance of the afternoon. Consequently, I have had no time to eat lunch.

In a rush I arrive at the shopworn offices located off of West Burnside Street where the clinic is being held and my first client, an elderly lady, is already waiting nervously. I settle myself into the makeshift office that has been provided me and usher her in. She looks at me and, to my surprise, suddenly says, "Young man, you look hungry." Somewhat taken aback by this personal and very astute observation, I respond that I actually am somewhat hungry, not having had time for lunch. She scolds me as only a mother might, and I can almost hear the soft burr of my Scottish mother's stern voice of rebuke floating from her lips.

I show her to a seat and we begin our interview. She lives in one of the down-in-the-dumps apartments in Old Town and her only source of income is a modest Social Security allotment. For some reason the payments just stopped about two months ago. She has not been successful in learning why or how to get them started again. As a result she is desperate. She has no money to live on, her utilities are in arrears and about to be turned off, her rent is past due and she is being threatened with eviction. She has no relatives and has nowhere else to turn for help.

I make some telephone calls on her behalf and learn that there has been a glitch in her address at the apartment building, which is why her checks are being returned to the Social Security Administration's offices. With updated information I am told the checks will be sent out to her immediately. I also contact her landlord and the electric company to explain her circumstances and they both agree to withhold further action. The problems have been resolved and she thanks me profusely and leaves.

My next client is waiting and I usher him in and begin my second interview of the afternoon. About fifteen minutes into the session there is a sudden knock on the door. Somewhat perturbed at being interrupted in the middle of a consultation, I go to the door and open it. There is my elderly client, a small brown paper sack clutched in her hand.

"Here," she says, thrusting the bag into my hands. "I found fifty cents on the street." I must look bewildered. "It's a donut," she adds, "It's day-old but should still be good."

Before I can say a word of thanks or to protest her generosity, she is gone. In all my years of law practice, I don't recall ever receiving a more generous fee, or enjoying a more nourishing lunch. I may not even need dinner.

EVEN ALONE

EVEN ALONE WE ARE NEVER ALONE. SHE IS THE AIR we breathe, her form a kind of darkness that fills us with her leaving. At night she rattles the door, begs forgiveness, holds us in her arms. We dream of morning.

It has been months. We have learned the dance of grace. A small bird comes to the feeder. In the winter air he sits alone, searching. We watch his progress, know the uncertainty by which he lives. Soon it will be spring again, an anniversary of sorts, a rounding off of time. We reach out. The bird is gone.

In this place, this place of stones, this place where death lives, where everyone is young, where time holds us like the children we are, we gather to say again, "We love you," to see again the disappearing face, to trace the distance by which we live, and then the silence.

CHAPTER THIRTY-FIVE

It is Thanksgiving. Once again we are up at the cabin, the entire family. Same as last year. The kids are skiing up at Timberline and Linnette and I are tending to the fire and having some quiet time together.

A year has passed since our last Thanksgiving celebration. We have survived the passage of time. A year and a half since she left us. In some ways we are healing. In other ways, we are as raw as ever. Today we will again go to the Resort at the Mountain for the buffet dinner and again listen to the Christmas carols as local high school students dressed in Dickens's costumes wander among us celebrating the beginning of the holiday season. It will again be bittersweet.

Aaron is back at the University of Washington. Jennifer is still involved with her graduate program at Portland State. Linnette still takes herself to work each workday. I still head off to the office or the courthouse.

As we wait for the kids to return I am perusing the

current issue of the Oregon State Bar monthly magazine, *The Bulletin.* My mind wanders over the classified ads. And then I see it. An ad for a Volunteer Lawyer Project Coordinator for Marion-Polk Legal Aid in Salem, Oregon. I read it several times. What if? What if, I wonder?

Later after our dinner at the Resort we are again sitting around the cabin enjoying the warmth, both of family and the great stone fireplace. There is little conversation. Mostly we sit quietly watching the fire burn down to ash. The surrounding forest is losing itself to darkness. The little cabin is a world unto itself.

During the night I get up and return to the living room and sit alone in the dark. Aaron and Barb are asleep in their sleeping bags, set out in front of the fireplace. Jenn and Ben are up in the sleeping loft. I can hear the rhythm of their breathing. Linnette is in the bedroom gently snoring.

I am thinking about the ad for a volunteer coordinator. What if I were to apply? What if I were to simply close down my practice that I have spent twenty years building and go to work for a legal aid program in Salem, fifty miles away? And for a modest salary at best?

It's a crazy idea. And what would Linnette say? Just that. Ron, you're nuts to even think of that. Look what you would be giving up. And I say, what would I be giving up? What might I gain?

Sunday, late afternoon, as we make our return trip home, and we are alone for the first time in several days, I mention the ad to Linnette. I try to sound as casual as I can. She reacts as I had anticipated. "Are you nuts?" "Look at the commute?" "Look at what you would be giving up?" We lapse into silence. I put the thought behind me.

But Monday morning comes and the charade begins again. I put on my lawyer suit and head off. Nothing has changed.

Later, at lunchtime, I am standing alone by Allison's gravesite. I have a sandwich with me, and a cup of coffee. The weather is unusually mild and the sky is blue. A lovely late November day.

"What do you say, Sweetie?" I ask. I look out over the green lawns with their row after row of engraved markers. The finality of it all overwhelms me.

A NIGHT ON THE MOUNTAIN

A NIGHT AT THE CABIN. WE SIT IN THE DARK, SILENT AS trees, and like trees, we sway gently. I want to tell you how much I miss her. But you know me too well. "She is everywhere we are," you say. And as you speak the night we are deepens, spreads itself deeper and deeper into the forest, into the lives of animals and stones.

CHAPTER THIRTY-SIX

It is later the same week. The thought of a change haunts me more and more. It is late in the day. I sit at my desk looking out at the parking lot, the same gray color that seems now to be my life. What do I really have to lose, I think. I could at least apply. If it isn't for me, I don't have to accept it. And they may very likely not want me, an aging lawyer, almost over the hill. Or so those young, whipper-snapper legal aid lawyers might think.

So that evening I begin to put together a resume. Something I haven't done for many, many years. What to say? How to capture the twenty-plus hectic years of private law practice in a few terse paragraphs. At one time I was in personnel work for Multnomah County. I saw literally hundreds of resumes over the years. I try to think back on what impressed me and what left me unimpressed.

Finally I put something together that seems to be adequate. I type out a letter on my old Mac and send it, along with the resume, off to Marion-Polk. I don't tell Linnette what I have done. I may never hear from them. Why upset her for nothing. I feel deceitful.

Less than a week later I get a phone call at the office from Michael Keeney, the Director of Marion-Polk County Legal Aid Service. They want me to come down to Salem for an interview. I agree to do so and we set a date and time. Michael is warm and friendly and we have a nice but short conversation. Now I am going to have to come clean with Linnette and tell her what I am up to.

That evening after dinner I break the news to her. She is not particularly pleased and raises the same questions we had both raised before. Are you nuts? But, as usual, she has more insight into what is going on with me than I do. We just sit quietly for a while drinking coffee and then head to bed. I have a restless night. She does too.

—

It is the first Friday in December and I am on my way to Salem for the interview. The legal aid offices are on the second floor of a shabby building on the edge of downtown, what appears to be a renovated motel. There I meet with Michael and the office paralegal, Leslie. The interview is very relaxed. A few of the usual questions. It has been a long time since I was on the opposite side of an interviewing panel. More than anything, they seem curious as to why I am interested in making such a drastic and dramatic change. Especially given the equally dramatic drop in income.

I make no mention of Allison or our loss. I don't want to bring that into the conversation at this point. Rather I tell them of my increasing involvement with the pro bono projects in Multnomah County and the fact that we are practically empty-nesters now and I want to redirect my contributions to the profession in what years I have remaining. My answer is true as far as it goes And they seem satisfied.

—

It is Wednesday of the following week. I get a phone call from Michael and he offers me the job. I don't know quite what to say. In a sense, I am taken by surprise. The reality of what I have done is now staring me in the face. I ask if he can wait until the following Monday for my answer. He says they can, and we end the conversation.

That weekend, as usual, Linnette and I head to the cabin. Again, it is just the two of us. No plans. Just a hike, perhaps. A quiet dinner on Saturday night. Nothing out of the ordinary. But I am even more quiet than usual. What can I say? How do I approach this? I have not even made any decision in my own mind. I am looking for permission. Will I find it?

It is Saturday evening. We have had a nice dinner at the Log Lodge, including a couple of gin and tonics, and we are sitting in front of the fireplace. I tell Linnette what has transpired. She says nothing. She has already made it clear she doesn't think much of the idea of giving up the business I have spent so many years building from scratch. And I am certainly not yet that close to retirement age. I still need to earn a living. What will this mean to our plans for retirement? What will be the financial costs? The points she is making are important ones. It could be like stepping off a cliff.

Finally she says, "Sleep on it. Whatever you decide you need to do is fine with me." I'm not sure if she really means that but she knows how the practice at present is eating me alive. She has seen it in my face for months now. Heard it in my voice. I nod and we kiss and head to bed, where I toss and turn late into the night.

About 2 a.m. I get up so as to not disturb her further and sit in the dark of the living room. The fire has burned itself out and is just a pile of gray ash. It is deathly quiet. There in the depth of the silence of the cabin I make the decision to accept the offer. The deed is done. I return to bed and sleep soundly until morning.

Over breakfast at the Alpine Hut I tell Linnette my decision. She nods her acceptance. Yes, the deed is done. For the first time in a year and a half I have something to look forward to. Something to live for. A tremendous weight is lifted from my shoulders. Linnette has allowed me to save my life. I am again in her debt.

THE CABIN IN WINTER

IT COULD ALWAYS BE LIKE THIS, WINTER AND THE DEEP cold invading our lives, wind and the swirls of snow taking their toll. We sit, you and I, husband and wife, father and mother, before the fire, before the altar that is our past. Where do we go? How do we bind thsee wounds that bind us, prisoners of loss to a dead child?

Now that winter is here we walk out into the snow, into the deep drifts of silence, up the road to the river. That silence hangs between us, not silence really, just the absence of words. It has been so long. The seasons click into place their hard time. We do only the simple things. On this mountainside we draw her breathe, like a third body, into our lungs. We fashion a future out of air, out of memory.

CHAPTER
THIRTY-SEVEN

It is the first Monday in January. I am reporting to work at Marion-Polk Legal Aid in Salem. This is the first "job" I have held in over twenty years. I am a bit nervous. The commute from our home in the Parkrose neighborhood of Portland took about an hour. It was not as bad as I had anticipated. Actually it gave me a little time alone to think. Later I will be able to form a carpool with other employees also coming from the Portland area.

Michael welcomes me as I enter the reception area. He takes ma around and introduces me to the staff. First Rafa, our receptionist. Then Carla our office manager. Then Leslie and Oralilla, our paralegals. Then Claudia our secretary. And finally the professional staff, David, Peter, Chris, Carolyn, Maryhelen and Chuck. With the exception of Peter, they are all relatively young, at least compared to me, and all of them are relatively recent members of the Bar. Thus they may benefit from the experience of older attorneys like me, for guidance. Been there, done that.

It is also the first day of work for David, the new Director of Litigation. He is from Florida where he worked in their legal aid system for a number of years. He is a new Oregonian. So we are getting our orientation together. He too lives in the Portland area.

The staff is welcoming and I am shown my office, a small but adequate room with a view of the street below. Not exactly the "corner office' but good enough for my needs. There is a scarred and aging desk, an executive chair that leans precariously to one side, two straight-back side chairs and a small bookcase. I have brought with me my various certificates of Oregon State Bar membership to hang on the wall positioned so as to be easily seen by clients, my so-called "ego" wall.

Michael calls a case review meeting of the professional staff to orient David and me to the daily routine. At weekly case review we gather to go over everyone's caseload and discuss strategies for moving forward. Each attorney presents his or her cases and we discuss options. David will be leading these weekly meeting in the future as Director of Litigation. But for today, Michael takes the lead.

Later Michael and I discuss my particular area of responsibility, to strengthen and expand the Volunteer Project. I will be reaching out to the local bar for volunteers to staff pro bono legal clinics that we have already formed in Salem, West Salem, and Monmouth, a small city to the west in Polk County. We hope to add other clinics as needed and as volunteers become available. I hope to initiate new opportunities and concepts as well. At this point I know few of the local State Bar membership.

These free clinics each meet once a week for several hours during which volunteer attorneys meet with scheduled low income clients for initial interviews regarding legal issues they are facing. Some issues will be resolved with the interview while others may need some follow up, in which a case a file is opened and the attorney carries on with it to its resolution. I have handled such clinics myself for some time in Multnomah County and am familiar with how they are structured.

It is my first day. For the first time in months I feel at ease. I sit in my lopsided chair and stare down at the street below. The office is on the edge of the downtown area and I can see a neighborhood of stately private homes directly across the street from me. Large, older homes representative of old Salem.

This is my new world. I have had no time to worry about my own ills. Having been in private practice for so many years, I am unaccustomed to being part of a large office with everyone having defined responsibilities. But it feels good. While I am "the old guy" among the young and enthusiastic, I feel somehow like I am finally at home. At last I am where I need to be for the first time in a very long time.

CHAPTER
THIRTY-SEVEN

THE DAYS ON THE NEW JOB ARE LIFESAVERS FOR ME. THE COM-mute has become even more enjoyable as I now carpool with David and Maryhelen. We meet at a K-Mart parking lot just off the 1-5 at Tualatin. We take turns as to who drives. David and I are the "newbies" but Maryhelen has been with the office for a couple of years. Thus we can be schooled in all the office intrigues, which don't' seem to be too many. David has many stories about legal aid practice in Florida. But I am the one with the most years in the law business generally and they pick my brain con-stantly. David is well experienced but, of course, new to Oregon law and practices.

After several months on the job I learn that one of the staff attorneys is planning to leave to teach English in China and that her slot will be open. She has been han-dling the Senior Law contract for the office. The contract is with the Area Agency for the Aging and it makes our program responsible for providing certain legal services to the elderly. It is an important part of the overall mission. Michael takes me aside and asks me if I would be interested in adding that responsibility to my present workload. It would increase my salary, which would be helpful. Given that I am the "old guy" in the office and would relate more easily with the older clients, plus my experience in private practice doing much of the same sort of work, I am an obvious choice. I agree and soon I find myself taking on more responsibility.

Meanwhile the Multnomah County Volunteer Lawyer Project, which has been sponsoring a legal clinic in Gresham, Oregon serving the growing Hispanic population, where I volunteered before coming to work in Salem, is looking for a consultant to work with a down-town Portland law firm which has agreed to take over responsibility for that clinic, providing its own attorneys to do the pro bono work, and paying the administrative costs as well. They will only do it, however, if they have access to an experienced poverty law lawyer to supervise their more inexperienced lawyers. I am asked to take on the contract. It would mean meeting with the clinic one evening a week in Gresham and providing periodic case review with the individual attorneys as needed, which I can do on late Friday afternoons.

Thus I now have not one but three jobs, combined into what is now really fulltime work. And all in an area that actually excites me. Excites me for the first time in many months. And it pleases Linnette as I will be making more money, however still comparatively modest. Later I will be asked to do consulting work from time to time as well for the National Legal Services Corporation helping to audit the 300 plus local legal aid programs thorough out the country on a per-audit basis.

Little by little opportunities are opening up. My risk in giving up my private practice has miraculously seemed to work out for the good. Good for me, and hopefully, good of my clients as well. A win/win. Our weekend trips to the cabin are becoming for me, more a time for a needed rest from a busy week than a time to rebuild my life. I am slowly evolving into my new self.

However, only last week, as I drove home from the office by myself I suddenly burst into tears. I realized I had not thought of Allison once that day. How could I? The sense of guilt was overcoming.

CHAPTER
THIRTY-EIGHT

IT IS MARCH. ANOTHER BIRTHDAY WITHOUT HER. WE DECIDE
to make a visit to our special bench. Our special bench sits,
no matter the season or the weather, just off the asphalt
path that winds down through the forested hills of Mountain Park, where we now live, bordering Spring Creek.
Over time its wood planks have weathered to a silvery
brown, lighter in color and shinier than its original cedar
finish. The small brass plaque remains as it was, however.

"In Memoriam, ALLISON ELAINE TALNEY,
1965-1988.
'I will speak to you, not with words,
but with movement, a dance of wind."

This bench and its plaque were placed here soon after
Linnette and I moved to Mountain Park, when we first
walked this path and felt movement in the surrounding
fir trees, their limbs gently swaying in the breeze, and the

leaves of maple trees drifting down in their slow dance around our feet. It was fall, and it seemed such a mysterious and unseen force. We stopped to rest and quickly felt our daughter's presence. It was here on this curve of path we asked permission to place this bench in her memory.

It is located about halfway downhill, between where we live and the local shopping center. Folks coming up from the New Seasons Market, along the creek and through the woods, carrying their heavy bags of groceries can stop here and rest, as we often do. From time to time as I walk down the path and past the bench an elderly man or woman will be sitting there holding sacks of groceries and enjoying a few moments of respite. They will nod and smile, seemingly grateful for this small oasis but unaware of what connection I might have, if any, to the bench.

We too have rested here many times. Her death is farther behind us now, but with us always in ways the world will never see. Our lives are strangely normal. We live each day in her absence, caught in this space between belief and disbelief. Knowing she is gone but never far.

And now it is this bench that remains. This bench that has become such a symbol of our new life. This is our quiet place where the breezes at all times of the year move the limbs of the evergreens, making them sway to her unseen presence, where maple leaves in the fall still drift down and cover the ground at our feet. Where birds in springtime build their nests, and where in summer squirrels gather nuts, preparing for winter's blast. Here we can sit, husband and wife, father and mother, still together, watching the seasons change, time move on and on in its own slow way. A resting place. A place where stillness lives between the past and the future. If only I had known our future I would have held her and not let go. But I did, and she was gone.

"*I will speak to you, not with words but with movement, a dance of wind.*"

I would have held her and not let go. I would have held her forever.

EPILOGUE

*"The wound is the place where
the the light enters the body."*

Rumi

I<small>T IS EVENING ON THE MOUNTAIN</small>. W<small>E SIT IN THE DARK CABIN</small>, husband and wife, alone, or so it would seem. The outside spotlight shines illuminating the front deck and deep into the forest beyond. Although it is April, it is snowing, and large flakes are drifting down through the shafts of light. It is rare to see snow at our elevation this late in the year. It seems like a gift. There is now about an inch.

It is April 8th, to be exact. We are searching back through the years, as we always do on this date. It is a date we would sooner avoid, but still we cling to it desperately as it represents our last contact with her in life. As with each anniversary of the death of our daughter, we took flowers to the cemetery. We stood on this day in a gentle spring rain by her grave site and looked out over the West Hills at the mist gathered among the trees on a distant slope. And later, exhausted by the continuing reality of her loss, we came up to the cabin, our place of refuge on Mount Hood.

And now that night has fallen Linnette is moving about, tending the fire, lighting candles on the mantel. This cabin remains our retreat since soon after Allison's death. We still call it our "bleeding place," a place where we can come to be alone. A place locked in primordial stillness, where we can come to laugh and cry, and scream our rage, when necessary. It is here, in this sanctuary of disbelief, where we still reach across the darkness that now holds her and touch again the child we will never touch again, and hear again the voice that we will never hear again.

It is here we have learned over time the meanings of renewal and regeneration. It is here, deep in the forest, comforted by tall pines and mountain laurel, that we have discovered the lessons of spring, that with each new year we are inevitably restored. That with each new season insects begin to move about, migratory birds return, wildflowers bloom, and mushrooms again burst into being in the most improbable places and under the most difficult circumstances.

It has taken so long. But the journey is far from over. Especially on certain days. We have had other losses over the years. Buried others we loved. But none so difficult, so untimely, or so senseless. None that required us to restructure the calendar, to recalculate our lives, to write anew our private history.

The death of our child has brought us to this. It is not wisdom, to be sure. It is not even acceptance, despite the passage of time. It is, however, a kind of growth that, tragically, would not have been possible in any other way. It is nothing we would have sought out. Not insight we would have wanted. But we have learned the kind of strength that enables the crippled to finally walk and the blind to find another way of seeing.

And so we sit watching the late snowfall, watching the deck slowly disappear beneath its accumulation of flakes. There is now a lone candle left burning on the mantel above the great stone fireplace. Its scent drifts out across the room. Its image flickers on the wall. I turn off the outside light. Linnette blows out the candle.

"And we will whisper 'daughter,' 'sister,' out upon this gathering of darkness."

THE END

ABOUT THE AUTHOR

RONALD TALNEY HAS PUBLISHED FIVE BOOKS OF POETRY, the latest being "A Secret Weeping of Stones, New an Selected Poems," from Plainview Press, as well as two novels and numerous personal essays and op-ed columns. In 1985 he wrote the official dedication poem for the statue, PORTLANDIA, the second largest copper-beaten statue in the country, second only to the Statue of Liberty. He writes a regular column for the Lake Oswego Review newspaper called "My World." He lives in Lake Oswego, Oregon with his wife Linnette.

ACKNOWLEDGEMENTS

I WOULD LIKE TO THANK ALL THOSE WHO HAD THE COURAGE TO come into our lives during these most difficult times and who supported us in our journey. This includes, of course, our family members, who suffered this loss with us, and also long-time friends, new friends and colleagues. And my special, heartfelt thanks to Professor James Elkins of the West Virginia University School of Law, and Editor of the Legal Studies Forum where substantial portions of this manuscript were originally published. And to Louise Mengelkoch for her eagle-eye in going over this manuscript to make needed corrections.

And finally, above all, to my wife and life partner, Linnette, for her willingness to allow me to revisit this most difficult journey in our personal history and to, in a sense, walk again the path we were made to walk. I am forever grateful for her love and support.